This book is dedicated to all those who told us
their secrets, knowing that we'd pass them on to you,
our readers.

CONTENTS

𝒾NTRODUCTION

There was a time when all the laws humans thought they needed could be reduced to a list of ten commandments. "Thou shalt not commit adultery" was one of them. Since then, many societies have regarded adultery as a crime. Usually, it is defined as sexual intercourse between two people, at least one of whom is married to another. In the last few decades, most laws imposing criminal penalties for adultery have been repealed. Until then, a large percentage of the population was engaging regularly in felonious acts.

Most of the time these acts remained unpunished, the perpetrators unprosecuted. Perhaps this was because so many of the lawmakers, prosecutors, and judges who were charged with enforcing our laws were adulterers themselves. Sex outside of marriage is, after all, a common phenomenon.

Adultery is not a product of the sexual revolution generally attributed to the 1960s and 70s. It has been happening as long as humans have walked the earth. King David's affair with Bathsheba was his undoing. His son Solomon, although legally married to seven hundred wives, also had affairs with three hundred concubines.

As a result of recent cultural changes, many couples are now living together openly in relatively permanent relationships, without the benefit of ceremonial marriage. But not much else has changed from biblical times. Men and women still tend to seek sex outside their domestic partnerships.

There are probably as many reasons for this as there are people. Some find the monotony of monogamy tedious or boring. Others claim that the partner with whom they have chosen to make a life is simply unable to supply all the sex they need. Many offer explanations that are deep or mysterious, claiming that sex outside their main relationship strengthens the bond between themselves and their partners, or that having an affair restores their sense of youth and excitement.

Maybe all these explanations should be taken with a grain or two of salt. What really counts is that, whether motivated by lust or emotional need or boredom or a hunger for additional stimulus, sex outside a committed relationship occurs and will continue to occur. It has been going on since the Earth began turning and will continue as long as the sun rises and sets. Not even the threat of death from a sexually transmitted diseases has stopped or will stop people from seeking sex partners in addition to their mates.

We have previously published five books about the sexual behavior of real people. Our work has given us a reputation for being interested, nonjudgmental listeners. This encourages large numbers of people to approach us with stories about their sexual experiences. We conduct many interviews and discuss sex with many people, but never as psychologists or sociologists or any other kind of "-ologists." We just listen attentively and report on what we've heard.

In this book, we have collected stories of people in permanent relationships who maintain sexual affairs outside the pale of those domestic partnerships. We have never put much stock in the conclusions reached by researchers who take sexual surveys or conduct interviews. There are several reasons for this.

First, many researchers begin with a conclusion and then hear only the statements that support it. Worse, they may have a conscious or an unconscious tendency to frame their questions in a way that communicates that conclusion to the people they are interviewing. This tips off the subject to the answer that is expected and encourages him or her to give it.

Second, even a researcher who approaches the subject with an open mind will be hampered by the fact that most people are unwilling to talk about their sex lives. This makes it impossible to find a random sampling on which to base conclusions. Instead of receiving information from a cross section, the researcher receives information only from people who enjoy talking about their sexual activities. There is much to be learned from this group of conversational exhibitionists, but the information is too skewed to permit valid conclusions about the general population.

Finally, those who are willing to discuss their sexual activities rarely do so with complete honesty. We have discovered this by comparing answers to some of our standard questions. For example, when asked how often she or he has sex, an informant may say, "At least three times a week." But later, when asked to describe his or her most recent sex experience, the same informant may begin by saying, "It was about three weeks ago."

Recognizing all this, we make no attempt to analyze the reports we receive or to confirm their accuracy. We do not draw any broad conclusions and suggest none to our readers. If our informants offer reasons for their behavior, we pass those reasons along, although we recognize that they are not always honest or correct. We believe that we can all learn from the interpretations, even false interpretations, that people place on their own behavior.

So, although we have separated the stories in this book into chapters based on the reasons our subjects gave in explaining their activities, we have organized those chapters to make for interesting reading, rather than to reflect any conclusions about what reasons are most important or most common. We recognize that the true reasons may have to be found between the lines. This we leave to you. In reading about the sexual conduct of the people in this book, we are sure that you will see, as have we, that sex outside a committed relationship sometimes damages or destroys that relationship, and sometimes helps or strengthens it. We hope that working to understand the sexual behavior of others will lead you to a better understanding of your own sexuality.

$\mathcal{S}$ECRET
SEX

1

IT'S GOOD FOR MY MARRIAGE

PEOPLE SEEKING LOVE IN THE WESTERN WORLD SEEM to have marriage, or at least a relatively permanent domestic partnership, as their goal. From our earliest childhood games, we are conditioned to expect to spend our adult lives with a single mate of the opposite gender. The varying disciplines of social science offer a multitude of reasons for this, ranging from the need for tribal males to feel secure about females tending hearth and home while they are out hunting or making war, to the requirement of a readily discernible lineage for stabilizing the concept of inheritance. Whatever the reason, it is clear that each of us is expected to form a single alliance with another person for life.

Divorce statistics show that this expectation is frequently unrealistic. Again, the social scientists offer a variety of explanations for why this is so. Some explanations are far-fetched, while others are plausible. We feel that the only one that is certain is sexual. After seeing, touching, and coupling with the same partner's naked body for a period of time, a person tends to grow bored and to hunger for change.

Self-styled experts have come up with dozens of ways to prevent monotony from killing a marriage. A glance at the magazine racks in any supermarket or at the self-help shelves in any bookstore will present many examples. Depending on the publisher's point of view, solutions may involve couple's therapy, exotic vacations, wardrobe suggestions, or even a new recipe for strawberry cheesecake.

This chapter contains stories told by people who claim that they have rescued their marriage from the doldrums of sameness by engaging in extramarital affairs. Nelson has made a habit of it, experiencing the heartbreak of two failing relationships before hitting upon what he believes to be a formula for success. Glenda fell into an affair without intending to do so and later discovered that it brought a new spark to her marriage. We don't know how their experiences will end, and we don't recommend their strategies for anyone else. We do think it might be helpful, though, to see the positive side of their secret sex lives.

KEEPING IT ALIVE

Nelson, who is about forty years old, is a professor in a graduate business program at a state university. He stands six-foot-one, with a lean muscular build that he maintains by working out regularly at the university gym. His medium-length blond hair frames his light-complected face, giving him a youthful yet scholarly appearance. His bright green eyes seem to look right through the person to whom he is speaking, giving one the feeling that Nelson is performing a careful appraisal as he talks.

My work puts me in a position to make contact with lots of intelligent young females. My classes are full of them—women in the world of business who think that an MBA will help them advance from middle to upper management overnight. They admire me. They look up to me. That makes them easy conquests.

In some ways, this has made my life very pleasant. In others, it has been the root of a great deal of heartbreak. I'm on my third wife at the moment. My first two marriages failed because I got too involved with attractive students who wanted to idolize and mother me all at the same time. Neither of my first two marriages lasted more than five years. I'm hoping this one will be different.

The first time I got married, I was twenty-five and just starting my teaching career while working toward my Ph.D. in finance. Anna was a colleague, also teaching in the business department. She was a couple of years older than I was, but very, very sexy. When she was in front of a class, she wore severe, dark suits and had her hair pulled back into a sexless bun. But at home, she was a tigress. She would dress for me in the laciest, most erotic lingerie I could imagine and would captivate me by stripping slowly while I sat on the bed and watched her, getting more aroused and more excited by the minute.

Our marriage was hot for the first three years. Then it started cooling off. One afternoon I found myself in a motel room with one of my students, killing time between classes with an idle fuck. A week or so later, I went with another. After that it became a regular occurrence.

Anna probably suspected it, but she never said anything about it. We were beginning to lose sexual interest in each other. After a little more than four years of marriage, we hardly ever had sex with each other anymore. I wouldn't be surprised if she was taking on an occasional student herself. Eventually, I found myself involved in a serious affair.

Britney was one of my students. She was a good five years younger than I and single. At first we started seeing each other for recreational sex. Before I knew it, I became emotionally attached to her. When I saw her talking to her male classmates, I actually became jealous. Soon I had myself convinced that I couldn't live without her.

My divorce from Anna was relatively painless and without rancor since we had lost all interest in each other anyway. After a decent waiting period, Britney and I were married. She was very different from Anna. She was the same person publicly as she was privately. Sexy, but in a wholesome sort of way. She wore short skirts that showed off her shapely legs and tight sweaters that accentuated the curves of her ample breasts. Underneath, she wore sensible white cotton undies.

Our nights were filled with passionate lovemaking, but somehow it never reached the levels of excitement I had known with Anna. After about a year and a half, I started taking students to motels again. At first it seemed to put sparks into my marriage. I'd come home following an afternoon rendezvous, my head filled with recollections of the girl I had been with and the things I had been doing with her. When Britney and I went to bed, I would perform some of the same acts on her body, but I'd be thinking of the other woman. For a few more years, this managed to keep our marriage alive.

Then, when I met Caroline, my relationship with Britney started to pale hopelessly. Right from the start, Caroline was more than an afternoon fuck to me. To begin with, she was twenty-four, a little more than ten years younger than I, and satisfying her made me feel like a real sexual athlete. Her sexual experience was pretty limited, so it seemed that almost everything I did was happening to her for the first time. Whenever we went to bed together, I felt I was with a virgin.

I fell in love with her almost immediately. But the idea of having two marriages go down the tubes, one after the other, was horrifying to me. I tried to breathe life into my relationship with Britney. I worked hard at turning myself on so that I could perform with her. I just didn't have it for her anymore, though.

She noticed. At first she was solicitous, asking me repeatedly about my health and suggesting that I see a doctor about my flagging sex drive. Then she became hurt, sensing that she wasn't exciting my sexual interest anymore. Inevitably, she started questioning me about my activities, accusing me of fooling around. She called it "cheating." Funny, I had never thought of it in terms of that word.

I denied the affair for about a year, but I was becoming more and more enmeshed in it. Caroline was starting to make demands, putting pressure on the relationship. She said she wasn't going to hang around while I worked things out with my wife. I had to make a decision. It was either her or my marriage. I chose her.

Telling Britney I wanted a divorce was no picnic, as it had been with Anna. She was furious and shattered, both at the same time. She cried for days, sobbing bitterly, even wailing at times. It broke my heart to see her in such pain. I just couldn't help her, though. It was over. Soon after our divorce, I married Caroline.

A few of my colleagues joked about the fact that I had gone from Anna to Britney to Caroline. They asked whether I planned to work my way through the alphabet. There turned out to be a certain prophecy to that.

Caroline is probably better suited to my sexual needs than either of my previous two wives. When I want sex, she is always ready, but she never initiates it and makes no erotic demands on me. She'll try just about anything I ask her to do, and she'll let me do anything I want to her sweet, pliant body. Even when she isn't in the mood, she'll let me have what I need, holding me lovingly while I enter her for the relief of my tensions.

We've been married for almost five years. I have to admit that the same three- or four-year syndrome has set in. A little more than a year ago, I started fooling around again. I told myself that it was only to keep my marriage stimulating, and the truth is that's all it's been. I went through three or four different casual partners—before meeting Denise. See, I really do seem to be going through the alphabet.

Denise is an absolute sex machine. I could tell that about her the first time I saw her, sitting in the last row in one of my classes. She kept looking at me and smiling lasciviously, licking her lips with the tip of a pointy pink tongue. After class, she strode up to my desk and said she wanted to discuss something with me in my office. I invited her to walk with me.

As we crossed the campus together, she managed to bump her hip against mine a half-dozen times. Each contact sent a little electric thrill through me. She said almost nothing, and I was feeling a little awkward. But the second we got to my office, that changed.

She closed the door behind us as she followed me in. Then, with no preamble, she said, "I know you've been fucking some of the other girls in your class and that's going to have to stop." I stared open-mouthed, fearful that I had fallen into the hands of one of those ardent feminists who fill every male professor who isn't gay with terror. Before I could respond, she stepped forward and placed her hand on my crotch. "From now on," she said, "this dick is for me."

I wondered whether I was being entrapped, but she removed all doubt when she swiftly unzipped my pants and pulled out my swelling erection. Without another word, she dropped to her knees and put her lips against it. Then she started sucking and licking me, forcing me to use all the strength of my will to keep from crying out in sheer pleasure.

While she worked on me, she opened her blouse and undid her bra, letting her voluminous breasts tumble free. I just stood there staring down at them as she tickled her own nipples with her fingers. She was completely in charge, which was a totally new experience for me. Within moments I was pumping my semen down her waiting throat, biting my lips to maintain silence. She drained me dry. Then she stood and kissed me, her lips sticky with my sap.

"You're mine," she said. "Every Thursday afternoon. I'll give you plenty more like I gave you just now. If you need any more than that, you can get it from your wife. Just make sure you stay away from the other girls."

There was something so forceful about the way she spoke that I felt powerless. And I liked it! This was a real switch. I had always been the aggressor in a sexual relationship, taking subtle advantage of the natural respect and admiration the students felt for me as their professor. Denise was treating me like some subservient creature, bound to do her bidding. In a way, she was relieving me of responsibility for my own actions. I had no choice but to obey her commands.

That night I was so hungry for Caroline that I kept her up for hours, making the most passionate and satisfying love either of us had ever known. I sucked on her nipples and plunged my tongue into her vulva, giving her orgasm after orgasm. I rode her until I came, and then rode her some more until my penis got hard all over again. I felt like a teenager, with an endless supply of sexual energy. By the time we fell asleep, the sun was only an hour away from rising.

The following Thursday, Denise stayed in the classroom, gathering her books until all the other students had drifted out of the room. Then she approached my desk and, in a hoarse whisper, gave me her address. Twenty minutes later, we were rolling around on her queen-size bed, coupling in every imaginable position, until I felt totally drained.

We spent most of the afternoon fucking, with very little time devoted to conversation. I did manage to learn that she was married to a medical graduate who was interning at a local hospital. His schedule was strict, so she could be absolutely certain of when he would and would not be home. I thought of asking her to let me come back the next day, but she made it very clear that our relationship was to be limited to one afternoon per week. She was still in charge.

I initially was disappointed, but as I reflected, I realized that it was a relief to know that she was married and that our affair would never become more than just a sexual release. It meant that my marriage was safe. Denise has remained in control, and I'm glad.

When we got together the following week, she kept all her clothes on except her underwear, pulling up her skirt to let me enter her, first vaginally and then anally. She knew exactly what she liked and wanted and knew how to get it from me. At the same time, she was giving me exactly what I liked and wanted.

Again, Caroline was the beneficiary of the sexual excitement that buzzed around in my head. We had fabulous sex that lasted half the night. We repeated the experience several times during the week. Caroline never knew that it was another woman who was stimulating me and making our sex life so intensely satisfying. I didn't feel the same kind of guilt I had felt before, because I knew my affair with Denise was motivated just by lust and nothing more.

I've continued seeing Denise once a week since then, missing only occasionally, when getting together with her was absolutely impossible. I find that my sexual interest in my wife is as strong as it ever was, and I truly believe that there is no danger of my third marriage going the way of the first two. Every time I meet with Denise, I tell myself that it's a good thing I'm doing. I've even convinced myself that I'm doing it for Caroline.

Sometimes I think I'd like to invite Denise to dinner so that Caroline can meet the woman responsible for preserving our marriage. But of course that's just a silly pipe dream. This works, but only so long as Caroline doesn't know that my secret sex life is what's keeping our relationship alive. Since our sex life is so prolific, she'll never imagine that I have someone else on the side. Everybody's different, and some people, like me, just need an outside interest to keep their marriage together.

OLD FRIEND

At thirty-one, Glenda is short and petite, with straight light brown hair that brushes gently at her slim shoulders. Her boyish figure is trim, with just a trace of bosom, and hips not much wider than her narrow waist. She has dark brown eyes that seem to close her thoughts off from anyone trying to peer inside her. Her work keeps her out in the field a great deal, giving her the kind of freedom she feels she needs.

My dad was a plumber, so I grew up in the trade. By the time I was twelve, I was helping him on jobs. It was good background for me. Now I have a pretty lucrative position as an estimator for a big plumbing contractor. We do work for the city and for lots of local developers. My job is to figure the prospective costs of a project so we can put in a competitive bid.

I always knew I wanted to work in the plumbing business, even when I was in college. That's where I met my husband, Rennie. We were both taking liberal arts courses, but Rennie says we were mostly taking up space. I was nineteen when we met. He's two years older than me. He sells insurance today and makes a pretty good living at it.

We had a whirlwind romance and got married after knowing each other for only a few months. It could have been a terrible mistake, but it wasn't. So far it's working out just great. I say that in spite of the little thing I have going on the side.

I know that's what you really want to hear about, so let me get right to it. Rennie and I have a good relationship, with a healthy amount of more-than-adequate sex. I don't have any complaints at all in that department. Getting into an affair was the last thing on my mind. For the first nine years of our marriage, I was perfectly satisfied. Actually, I still am.

About two years ago, I got a call from Earl. He's been a friend of Rennie's and mine ever since our college days. Not real close, but someone we would see socially maybe two or three times a year. Anyway, he called me at the office one morning, just as I was about to go out to estimate a job. He sounded very upset, so when he asked if he could meet me for a cup of coffee, I agreed.

As soon as I saw him, I knew there was something wrong. He looked like he hadn't had a decent night's sleep in days. When I asked him to tell me about it, he sighed and said that his marriage was on the rocks. He and his wife were fighting all the time, and she wanted him out of the house. He said he thought she might be having an affair of some kind and he just didn't know what to do.

I tried to give him a friendly pat on the shoulder, telling him that every marriage had its problems and that I was sure his wife wasn't cheating on him. I really didn't know anything about it, but it seemed to help. When we parted, he said he was going to talk to her and try to work things out. He asked if we could get together again sometime, and I said, "Sure."

He called me about a week later, and we met in the same coffee shop. Things were a little better between him and his wife, and he said he just wanted to thank me for my advice. A few days after that, he invited me to lunch. We started meeting on a fairly regular basis, just for conversation. Nothing more.

Sometimes he would tell me about fights he had with his wife. Other times, he would say that things were going well. On one occasion, he told me in rather explicit detail about the sex he and his wife had the night before. Part of me felt that I shouldn't be hearing all this, but another part of me enjoyed the description.

In fact, I found myself thinking about it later in the day. I pictured him naked and tried to imagine him and his wife making love. I found myself focusing on an image of his erection, trying to visualize how big and hard it might be. He was a muscular man, with huge hands, and I wondered if that stuff you hear about big hands and big cocks was true.

It seemed to be just idle fantasizing, but that night, when I was in bed with Rennie, I found myself becoming quite aroused by the images in my mind. I reached for my husband and began stroking his cock, feeling it leap into readiness. I pulled on it, guiding him into a position above me and directing him inside me. My eyes were tightly shut. All along, I was thinking about Earl.

The sex was good, but I found myself feeling a little guilty about my secret fantasy. I told myself that it was perfectly natural and that Rennie probably imagined some other woman, himself, while making love to me. But my curiosity was building. By the time I got together with Earl for lunch again, I was beginning to realize that our relationship was about to go a step beyond conversation. I knew it was significant that I had never once told Rennie about my meetings with him.

At this point, Earl and his wife had just separated. Since then, they've separated and reunited at least a dozen times. But that first time devastated Earl. He was renting a room in a residential hotel and was miserable. When we ordered lunch, he told me that his only consolation was meeting with me. I was the only person who really understood him.

As the waiter served the food, Earl's eyes filled with tears. "I don't think I can eat," he said. "I just want to go to my room and pull the covers over my head."

Without even thinking about it, I moved into the chair next to his and put my arm around his powerful shoulders in an attempt to comfort him. He was on the edge of a sob. "Come on," I whispered. "I'll walk you back to your place."

I can't even remember what happened next. All I know is that we were in his room and in each other's arms. At first he just hugged and clung to me, pressing the front of his body against mine. Rennie is about my size, but Earl is huge by comparison. He seemed to tower over me, enfolding me in the power of his embrace. At the same time he was helplessly childlike. I felt like Fay Wray in the clutches of an adoring King Kong.

It was like nothing I had ever felt before. Suddenly I was aware of his groin, unconsciously grinding against me. His cock was erect, pressing at the front of his pants and making me tingle with sexual anticipation. He bent to kiss me, and when our lips met, the heat was overpowering. I found myself fumbling with the front of his pants, hungry for his sex.

We literally tore each other's clothes off before falling onto the spongy mattress with our arms and legs intertwined. His mouth sought my throat and then my breasts, his lips nibbling so gently at my sensitive skin that I felt myself lifted to a peak of exhilaration.

I was so overcome with excitement and the thrill of his mighty physique that all I wanted was to abandon myself to his touch. I felt no guilt, no remorse, no regret. There was only this moment, only the two of us.

I felt his fingers moving over me, exploring my breasts, gently twisting my taut nipples. He was touching me in places no one but Rennie had ever touched me before, and in a way even Rennie never had. With one huge hand, he held both my breasts at the same time, while his other hand moved slowly and tantalizingly across my naked belly. When his fingers began tangling gently in the curls of my pubic hair, I moaned involuntarily.

I could feel myself opening to him, the lips of my vagina spreading and moistening to invite the entry of his fingers. He found my slit and began moving his whole hand against it, up and down, spreading my fluids to coat my entire groin. Involuntarily, my hips rolled in circles, as though trying to lift my sex up tight against his powerful grasp, but he kept the contact light and gentle.

I reached for his swollen cock. It was even bigger than I had imagined. I wrapped my hand around its thickness, feeling the warmth pulsing through the rich veins that bulged against its smooth surface. The head was a giant knob of hard yet yielding flesh, almost burning me with its heat.

Suddenly he was climbing over me, his face pressed to my open sex. I could feel his hot breath between my legs as the tip of his tongue began stroking the lips of my vagina. His swollen cock was poised over my mouth. I wanted to lick it, to feel its power pressing against my tongue. I took it into my mouth and began sucking on it.

It was huge, absolutely filling my mouth with its masculine strength. As I experienced the shape and flavors of his sex, my mind was drunk with the thought of having it enter my pussy. I was so small, and he was so large. Would he tear me apart?

He must have known what I was thinking. Moving with a delicate grace, he turned and knelt between my spread thighs. His cock was dancing in front of him as it pointed at my opening. I stared at it in wonder as he moved slowly forward and placed its tip against me. With his hand, he moved the giant knob up and down the length of my slit, coating it with the juices produced by my excitement.

Then, with an abrupt movement of his hips, he drove himself into me. I was exquisitely conscious of the membranes of my sex parting before his plunging onslaught. I was stretching and spreading to accommodate his massive force. There was no pain, no discomfort, nothing but sheer ecstasy. I wrapped my legs around his powerful thighs, welding my body to his. Together we rocked and writhed, our bodies locked in feverish union.

It seemed to go on forever. I could feel myself approaching orgasm and then deliberately withdrawing from it, trying to make the experience last as long as possible. He also managed to hold back his climax, until finally neither of us could stand the pleasure any longer. "Come for me," he grunted.

I did. It was the longest, most intense climax I had ever experienced. About halfway through it, his began. I could feel him swelling as he discharged all his pent-up fluid deep inside me. The thought that he was filling me with his hot semen excited me even more, further intensifying my orgasm. I think I screamed.

For a long time, we were silent, neither of us knowing quite how to deal with what we had just gone through. When he spoke, there was a note of apology in his voice. "Glenda," he began. "I didn't expect us to . . . I mean I . . ."

"Neither did I," I said softly. "But I'm glad we did."

I expected the guilt to set in later, but you know, it never did. I went back to my office and then went home early. I wanted to be sure to have a shower before Rennie got there. When he did, I was dressed in a sexy robe that he had bought me and had dinner waiting on the table. While we ate, I thought about the afternoon I had spent in Earl's bed and found myself becoming intensely aroused.

Rennie offered to do the dishes after dinner, but I just took him by the hand and led him to the bedroom. I threw open the robe and let him see that I was naked underneath it. I could feel his eyes fastening to my pubic triangle as he moved toward me. Somehow the idea of making love to my husband just a few hours after making love to another man had me incredibly turned on. I think I gave Rennie an evening he did not soon forget. I loved every second of it.

The memory of my encounter with Earl kept me turned on for weeks, causing me to drag my husband into the bedroom much more often than before. So when Earl called me again, asking me to meet him for lunch, I was more than eager. It didn't seem possible that we would ever have sex as fantastic as we had the first time, but I was dying to find out.

I was a little disappointed when Earl told me that he and his wife were back together again. I tried to be decent about it, telling him how glad I was, but the truth is I wasn't glad at all, because I thought that meant that it was over between us. Earl surprised me, though, shyly saying that he thought that afternoon had helped him to patch things up with his wife, and asking me if I'd ever be willing to do it again. When I told him I was willing to do it that very afternoon, he grinned like a happy child.

This time we went to a nice motel, where Earl checked us in while I waited in the car. Our sex was every bit as good as it had been that first time. Later that night, my sex with Rennie was better than it ever had been before.

Since then, Earl and I have gotten together every few weeks for sex in the afternoon. I don't think my marriage is the least bit threatened by it. In fact, I think it has been a definite improvement. I love Rennie and I love making love with him. But there's something about having a secret sex life with another man that makes our relationship all the more exciting.

2

PEEPERS

ACCORDING TO LEGEND, WHEN LADY GODIVA RODE
nude through the town of Coventry in eleventh-century England
to protest her husband's oppressive tax levies, the townspeople
expressed their gratitude by agreeing not to look. Only one man
violated the agreement. He was a tailor named Tom, who peeped
at the lady through his shop window and was struck blind as a
result. Since then, the name "Peeping Tom" has been given to any
person who sneaks an illicit peek at another's naked body.

Although the label bears a trace of contempt, the desire to look
at others with their clothes off is not an unusual one. Almost everyone enjoys seeing other naked humans. That is probably why the
nude body was a popular subject with sculptors and artists long
before Lady Godiva's ride.

Some people confine the voyeuristic urge to their own mates,
or to the centerfold pictures in popular magazines. Others like to
see live strangers in the nude. When both members of a couple
feel that way and openly acknowledge their feelings to each other,
they may be able to make peeping a part of their sex life together.
On the other hand, when one of the partners is unwilling to join
the other in these acts of visual stimulation, relationships outside
the domestic partnership are likely to develop.

Voyeurs frequently find that their experience is enhanced when it is shared with another. If their mates are not willing to participate, they may turn to people who are. That's what happened to Kevin and Rachel, whose stories are told in this chapter. Each was looking for someone with whom to enjoy voyeuristic activity. Neither was seeking an outside sex partner, but that's exactly what they found.

MOTEL

Kevin is thirty-three, but his hair is already graying at the temples, adding a dash of dignity to his already handsome looks. His blue-gray eyes are steely, giving him the appearance of quick wit and wisdom, an appearance that he insists is an illusion. He is tall and slender, with a charming smile that captivates and conquers. In spite of his dynamic personality, he has a tendency to disparage his own abilities.

I guess I've been a disappointment to my parents. They were hard-working folk who had dreams of my becoming a doctor or a lawyer or some other kind of professional. But I just wasn't cut out for study. If it weren't for this motel, I'd be lucky to scrape by on minimum wage.

My folks owned it for more than forty years. When they decided to retire, I stepped into a going business. They're gone now, but I think they could have continued operating the place right up till the end if they hadn't been so eager to set me up. They knew that my wife, Sandra, has enough business sense for both of us, so they didn't worry about me running the place into the ground.

Sandra and I have been married for six years. We're both the same age. Well, actually, she's a couple of weeks older than I am. We have fun together, but she's a lot more serious than me. Especially when it comes to finance. Our sex life is okay; we make love maybe two or three times a week.

I know my own failings. I don't have much of a head for business, so I leave all that to Sandra. I like working with my hands and stick pretty much to maintenance. The first thing I did when we took over the motel was start renovating the place. We've got a great location, surrounded by big trees and overlooking the lake, but it had been a while since the property got any tender loving care.

I patched a lot of cracked plaster and repainted all the rooms. There were bathroom doors that didn't close properly, and I planed them and rehung them until they were like new. I installed some modern fixtures where they were needed. Before long everything was nice and spiffy. My proudest accomplishment, though, was the wiring of one of the rooms.

Let me explain. For as long as I can remember, I've been a Peeping Tom. Voyeur, I guess they call it now. I never could resist sneaking a peek in an open window, or spying on people in various states of undress. The fact that my parents owned a motel made it easier, because it presented me with endless opportunities for that sort of thing.

I managed to fiddle with the drapes in a few of the rooms so that they wouldn't close properly. Then, when there were guests in those rooms, I'd creep up outside and get an eyeful. Sometimes, especially in the afternoons, when local cheaters tend to drop in for a quickie, I'd even see people having sex.

When the place became mine and I was renovating it, I hatched a plan for some real voyeurism. I'd seen plenty of movies about spies, with all their technology, and I'd seen ads on the Internet for miniature cameras. So I read up on them and ordered a few. While I was renovating the room at the far end of the building, I installed the little cams.

There's one in the bathroom and three in the bedroom, so I can see the guests no matter what they're doing. Oh, the cameras are hidden very cleverly, in smoke detectors, an alarm clock, and the grate of the air conditioner. I'm telling you this because you've promised to keep it a secret. No one must ever know the name of my motel, or have even the shadiest idea of its location.

I connected all the cameras into the wiring system, so I can view the images they pick up on a series of TV monitors in my little office. Not the motel registration office, but a little cubicle in the workroom where I keep all my tools. No one but me has reason to go in there. Not even the hired help has access to it. To play it safe, I keep it locked at all times.

As luck would have it, the evening after I got my spy system all set up, an attractive young couple checked in, and my wife assigned them to the peep-room. As soon as I realized that I had a couple of victims in my clutches, I ran to the workshop and locked myself in. I turned on the monitors and was amazed at how clear I could see everything happening in the room.

I watched the young woman taking a shower, while her husband walked around the bedroom, naked, waiting for her to come out. Then I saw them get into bed together and begin embracing. I could see his hands moving all over her and his lips traveling up and down her body. By the time he mounted her, I was so turned on I thought I would wet my pants.

This was too good to watch all alone. I considered buzzing my wife on the intercom and asking her to join me. But I hesitated, and as it turns out, I'm glad I did. What if she disapproved and made me take the system out? No, I'd better check it out first. In the meantime, I took out my dick and masturbated while watching the couple in the room.

The next day, I casually asked Sandra how she would feel about watching other people make love. At first she seemed quite puzzled by my question. She said she had no idea of what I meant. So I took it a step further and said I thought it would be a great turn-on for the two of us to watch some of the couples that come to our motel, especially the ones that come here just for sex.

My wife was appalled. First of all, she said, she thought it was sick and disgusting to even want to see such a thing. Then she said it would be a horrible invasion of privacy, just the thing that people come to a motel to have. I knew at once that I was in this alone. There was no hope of sharing the experience.

That didn't stop me from enjoying it, though. I kept track of who was checked into the peep-room. Whenever it looked like there might be some interesting action, I went to my tool shop and watched. Usually, I ended up masturbating, as I had that first time.

Then one day all that changed. I was adjusting the TV monitors to make the picture a little clearer when I noticed Marietta, the maid, working in the peep-room. She was vacuuming under the bed and as she bent forward, her dress hiked up in the back to show a nice pair of thighs and just a hint of white panties. I kept watching, hoping for some more secret views.

I noticed that as she dusted the night table, she seemed to be paying particular attention to the alarm clock. It was fastened to the tabletop so that it couldn't be stolen and, incidentally, so that the camera hidden inside would remain focused where I had pointed it. Marietta bent forward and inspected it closely. On one of the monitors, I could see her from behind. On another, I could see her eye moving closer and closer to the camera lens. Suddenly her face broke into a smile of recognition. I was terrified. Could she have caught me?

She immediately looked at the smoke detector and seemed to discover another camera. Then she glanced around the room, before staring intently at the air conditioner. She certainly seemed to have figured it out.

I didn't know what to do, so I did nothing. I thought if I could just stay away from her, the whole thing would disappear and I'd never have to confront it. I turned off the monitors and busied myself in the tool room. When I left my sanctuary, she was waiting outside. She wasn't being obvious about it. In fact, she was sweeping the pavement. But I knew this would be the confrontation.

I hadn't taken more than two steps out the door when she said in a very soft voice, "I know exactly what you're doing. Does your wife know, too?"

I stammered. "I don't know what you're talking about . . ." I attempted.

She just sneered. "Oh, yes you do," she said. "You're busted. I know all about it, and I'll bet Sandra doesn't. There's no getting away from it. Your only way out is to share the wealth."

I thought she was asking me for money. "What do you mean?" I stammered, trying to stall for time.

"I like the same things you like," she answered. "I want to see, too."

I looked at her closely. In a way, it was the first time I was seeing her. She was in her early thirties, short and a little stocky, with plenty of flesh in all the right places. She had worked for my parents ever since she was a teenager, but I hardly knew her. She wore a gray and black uniform dress, and somehow that was all I had ever noticed. Now I realized that she filled it out very nicely. She was actually a very desirable woman.

"Look," she said. "Your family has always been nice to me. I don't want to get you in any trouble. Just let me have a look, too. Are any of the other rooms wired? Where are your monitors? In there?" She pointed to my workshop.

There was no point in trying to deny it. She had me dead to rights. "No," I answered. "That's the only room with cams. And, yes, the monitors are in my shop."

"Suppose I meet you there tonight, then," she said. Her voice was soft but commanding. "Then we can share the view."

I had no choice. Meekly, I shrugged. "Okay," I said. "There's usually someone checked in there by eight o'clock or so. Why don't you come here then. Knock three times, so I'll know it's you."

That evening when I heard her knock, I nervously went to the door and unlocked it. "I've had my eye on things," she said. "There's a cute young couple in there. They look like they could even be on their honeymoon. Have you seen anything yet?"

"No," I said. "I've been waiting for you." The truth is, I was too nervous to turn on the monitors. I was afraid she might show up with the cops or my wife or something. "Anyway, I've been thinking of taking the cameras out."

"Oh, no," she said. "Don't do that. I've been peeking in windows as long as I've been working here. I've always known you were doing the same. But this is much better." She wasn't exactly rubbing her hands together, but that's how her voice sounded. "This is going to be good."

Encouraged, I flipped the switches. Immediately, the TV screens came to life. The bathroom monitor was dark, but the other monitors showed the couple in bed from three different angles. The woman was not much more than twenty, with a shapely athletic body. She was lying on her back with her breasts pointed at the ceiling. Her knees were pulled up and her thighs spread. The guy was lying facedown between her legs with his mouth fastened to her pussy. I didn't have sound, but I could practically see groans of pleasure coming from her mouth.

"Oh, yes," Marietta said. "This is hot."

I had watched dozens of couples on my spy system, but always alone. Having a woman there watching with me made the whole thing so much more exciting that I found myself rock-hard within seconds. I glanced at Marietta and could see her erect nipples straining at the front of her uniform. "Look at him eat her," she whispered.

Her words brought a drop of moisture from the tip of my dick. I could feel it staining the front of my pants. Marietta looked pointedly at the bulge my arousal was making. "Why don't you take it out," she said. "That's what you usually do when you're watching this, isn't it?"

"Yes," I admitted dumbly.

"Well, go ahead," she insisted. "I want to see it."

Embarrassed, but even more aroused, I unzipped my pants and extracted my hard-on. It was big and thick, and I was proud of it. Marietta smiled and began unbuttoning the front of her dress. "Let's fuck while we watch them," she suggested casually.

Within seconds, we were both naked. I sat in my swivel chair, facing the TV screens. She climbed into my lap with her back to me so that she, too, could see the monitors. Reaching down between her smooth, round, thighs, she took hold of my cock and guided it against the opening of her pussy. She was dripping wet and wide open. Peeking at the couple in the room was having the same effect on her that it had on me.

She raised herself slightly and then settled down again, impaling herself on my stiff cock. I could feel it sliding smoothly and effortlessly into the heated cavern of her pussy. We were both concentrating on the pictures flickering before us. Slowly, she moved her hips up and down, dragging the clinging membranes of her sex along the length of my cock. There was no pretense. We were both fascinated by the sights we were witnessing.

"Don't come in me," she whispered. "Give me a warning." Then, just as the words left her mouth, I could feel her belly begin to contract. She moved forward and back, up and down, around in little circles, as she reached a moaning, sobbing climax. I clenched all the muscles of my groin to hold back my own orgasm.

When I was sure she was done, I said, "I'm right at the edge." Swiftly, she moved off my lap, letting my cock slip out of her with a faint plopping sound. Immediately, she fell to her knees in front of me and took me in her hand. The second she touched me I started to come. My eyes were still glued to the monitors. She let the hot juice that spewed from my cock splash over her heaving breasts. Then, with her free hand, she rubbed it into her skin. We both looked up just in time to see the couple on the screens reaching their completion as well.

Marietta and I get together quite often now, but we have no illusions. We aren't in love. We aren't even in like. We aren't having an affair. I know very little about her, except that she's married to an auto mechanic. She knows very little about me. We both like it that way.

It just happens that we share a perversion. It's one that neither of our mates are willing to enjoy with us. So we enjoy it together. We love watching others having sex when they don't know they're being watched. But watching alone isn't anywhere near as satisfying as watching with a partner. The secret sex we have is just an expression of our mutual perversion.

NUDIST CAMP

Rachel is twenty-two years old and works for a courier service, delivering overnight packages. She is of medium height, a little on the chunky side, with broad shoulders and muscular arms. Her hips are wide and feminine, and there is something coquettish in her easy smile. Her long black hair is done with strings of beads in a way that complements her dark almond-shaped eyes and chocolate-brown skin. She giggles nervously as she talks.

Willard and I aren't married, but we've been living together for almost two years. He's about five years older than me. We'll probably get married someday. For now we're, what you might say, trying it out. So far, so good. Except for one little thing.

Willard and I are pretty compatible, especially in bed. He's a slow and thoughtful lover. I'm never dissatisfied after we make love. There's something about me that he just doesn't understand, though. I like looking at other people. Naked people.

I don't know what it is. I've always felt that way. Watching someone I don't know getting undressed or seeing a stranger in the nude just turns me on. I'll tell you something strange. I'm absolutely straight. I have no sexual interest in other women. Yet even seeing a naked woman turns me on. It doesn't make me want her. It makes me want a man. I can't explain it. The sight of skin just does that to me. Even female skin.

I think it started when I was in high school. I was pretty athletic, so I looked forward to the gym classes. One day I began to realize that it wasn't just the exercise that interested me. Before and after class, the girls would all be changing their clothes or showering in the locker room. There was nothing stopping me from looking to my heart's content. All I had to do was get into a conversation with somebody to give me a perfect excuse to look at her.

I enjoyed seeing them in their bras and panties. I especially loved it when they took off their underwear to get into their exercise clothes or take a shower. I was absolutely fascinated by the variety in the shapes of their breasts and their bottoms. Some had real hairy muffs; some were kind of sparse. A few were already doing bikini trims. Somehow, looking at all of them got me so excited that after class all I could think of was finding a boy to lie down with. Around the high school, I guess I was known as a loose girl.

I loved looking at naked boys, too, when I got the chance. I just didn't get the chance as often. Sometimes I managed to get a little peek into the boys' locker room when the boys were in there. But not anywhere as much as I would have liked to.

After I finished school, shopping became my favorite hobby. I'd go the department store when I knew the place would be really crowded, like on a Saturday, or when they were having a sale. I'd pick out a few garments and take them into the dressing room, just to give me an excuse to spy on the women trying on clothes in there. I almost never made an actual purchase.

When I first moved in with Willard, he couldn't understand why I managed to spend so much time shopping without ever buying anything. He also didn't understand why I always came home from a shopping trip so excited and so hot for his loving. He had enough sense to take advantage of it, though, and we had some really hot times.

I was still hungry to see a bunch of naked men, or even better, to see naked men and women at the same time. My route made me hotter for the idea. There's a nudist resort in my district, and I have to make a delivery there at least once a week. I was dying to get inside and have a real good look around. Every time I went there, though, someone met me at the gate to sign for the package. That was as far as I ever got.

I asked once about spending a day or a weekend there. They told me they only took couples. No problem. I was sure Willard would be as interested in seeing all that nudity as I was. Boy, was I surprised when he said he wanted no part of it.

It just wasn't his thing. He said he had no desire to walk around with a bunch of naked people, most of them probably flabby and old anyway. I tried explaining that even fat and ugly people turned me on when I saw them nude, but it was completely beyond his comprehension.

On days I had to deliver to the resort, I'd find myself getting all aroused as I drove up to the gate, just thinking about all the exposed flesh on the other side of it. Oh, if only I could find a way to peek inside. Or better yet, if only I had a partner who would go in with me.

Back at the dispatch office, it was a big joke that I had a nudist camp on my route. On days I got back late, the other drivers would all kid me and say stuff like, "Oh, Rachel must have been sunbathing today." Everybody got a big laugh out of it.

One of the drivers, a white guy named Mike, seemed to be a little more interested than the others. One afternoon, when there wasn't anybody else within earshot, he asked, "Seriously, Rachel, have you ever been inside that place?"

I don't know what made me open up to him. Maybe it was the fact that I couldn't talk to my own boyfriend about it. I answered, "No, they don't let me get past the gate. But I'd give anything for a look inside. I just love seeing nudies."

Mike sighed with understanding. "Me too," he said. "I can't help myself. The sight of a naked body drives me nuts. I inquired by phone once, but they said they only take couples. There's no way in hell my wife would go with me."

"Yeah," I said. "My boyfriend won't go, either. He thinks I'm nuts to even want to."

We stood together in silence, each contemplating the disappointment of having a partner who didn't understand us. I think we both got the idea at the same time, but it was Mike who said it first. "Why don't we go together, Rachel?" he said. "We could be a couple. I mean, just so we could get in. We could have an understanding. I mean, I won't bother you or anything. We could just go there together to see what we can see."

He spoke nervously. His idea made me nervous, too. "I don't know," I said hesitantly. "I wouldn't be able to tell Willard. That would make me feel kind of guilty, even though we wouldn't be doing anything wrong. No, I don't think I'd better."

All that night, I tossed and turned, thinking about Mike's proposal. I meant what I had said to him about not wanting to do anything that would make me feel guilty. But for some reason, I was struggling with the idea.

I realized that it would be easy for me to get away for the day. Willard and I have that kind of relationship. He goes off with his friends, and I go out with mine. We don't ask each other a lot of questions. What the heck, if he didn't want to try it, that shouldn't stop me. By morning, I knew I would go through with it.

When I told Mike, he was delighted. We arranged to meet and spend the following Saturday at the resort. He said he'd call and make reservations, if that was necessary. It wasn't. They told him all we had to do was show up at the gate and pay the day-use admission.

I was nervous when we met at the company parking lot that Saturday, thinking about all the sights that I would be seeing. We left my car behind and drove to the nudist camp in Mike's. As we were approaching the entrance, I realized for the first time that we wouldn't just be looking at naked people. We might have to be naked ourselves. I don't know how, but this thought had completely slipped my mind.

As if he knew what I was thinking, Mike said, "When I called, they told me that everybody who goes there is expected to be nude. So if you're not willing, better back out now."

I went through the motions of thinking it over, but I was really so excited by the idea of going through those gates and seeing all that naked flesh that nothing in the world would have stopped me. "I'm not backing out," I said defiantly.

We were met at the gate and admitted after Mike paid the fee. He identified us as Mr. and Mrs. Smith, but although the guard wrote that down, nobody really seemed to care much about who we were. We were given a little paper map and the key to a small changing room where we could remove our clothes and store them while we strolled around the park. On the way to the changing room, we saw at least a dozen naked people walking to and from the pool area or lying on lounge chairs on a broad green lawn to soak up the sun. I fought hard to keep from staring. I could tell that Mike was having the same problem.

There were a few awkward moments after we entered the changing room. It was so small that our bodies were practically touching all the time that we were in there. After taking a deep breath, Mike said, without further hesitation, "Well, I guess I'll do it." With that, he began stripping off his clothes.

At first I tried to be discreet and look in another direction. Then I remembered that we were both there to see naked bodies and there was no reason for me to pretend I wasn't interested. So I looked right at him while he undressed. His skin was kind of pale, but that didn't make it any less interesting to see. When his pants and his underpants came off, his cock sprang up, fully erect. It was an arousing sight for me.

"My God," he said. "I can't go outside like this."

"Don't worry," I reassured him. "I read about this. It'll go away when you step out of this room." With that, I took off my clothes, too. I could feel Mike's gaze on me as I stripped down to my crisp white bra and panties. He seemed to be acting involuntarily when his hand went to his cock and held it as I slipped out of my undergarments.

"Doesn't feel like it's going to go down," he said, wrapping a towel around his waist. Together we stepped out into the sunlight, blinking hard against the glare. All around us were naked people. Men and women together. Some were fat and old, as Willard had predicted. Others were young and athletic-looking. It didn't matter to me. The sight of each and every one of them was like a feather tickling my clit. I felt little flashes of excitement passing through me.

"Looks like you've got a hard-on, yourself," Mike said, casting a significant glance at my erect nipples. I looked down and saw them, dark brown and standing out like towers. "You can blame it on the breeze," he said with a smirk. "But I can't get away with that."

I could see that he was still hard under the towel. Nobody around us seemed to care, though. Maybe erections were not so uncommon at nudist camps. I looked around at all the other men, but not one of them had a hard-on. Seeing their dicks was a thrill anyway. Some were long and hung down their thighs like dormant creatures just waiting for a reason to come to life. Others, probably because the men had just gotten out of the pool, were shriveled and pulled back into their bodies so that only the rounded heads were showing. I had never before seen so many naked men at the same time.

There were women, too. I remember one who was very fat, with breasts that hung almost to her waist. From the corner of my eye, I could see Mike checking her over. Like me, he seemed just as interested in the unattractive ones as in the gorgeous ones. "Look at the tits on her," he whispered.

"Yeah," I murmured. "I've noticed. Her nipples are the size of jumbo prunes."

Mike groaned softly. "You have no idea how exciting it is for me to be able to share an experience like this with a woman. You're really something, Rachel."

"Look at that gorgeous guy's buns," I said, glancing in the direction of a body-sculpted man who was built like Atlas.

"Hmmm," Mike replied. "He's a Greek god." Embarrassed, he started to stammer. "I mean . . . I'm not that way or anything . . . I mean I'm not gay. I just can't help appreciating . . ."

I felt I had met my match. "Believe me," I said, laughing, "I understand completely. In fact, looking at the women has me just as turned on as looking at the men. I feel myself tingling all over and I'm starting to get wet. I don't know how I'm going to get through this day."

"I can make a suggestion," Mike said shyly. He waited, and when I said nothing, he continued. "We're both all turned on. We could go inside and satisfy each other. I don't mean getting all involved or anything. Just satisfy each other. You know what I mean?"

I knew exactly what he meant. In spite of all the promises I had made to myself about being faithful to Willard, I knew I was going to accept Mike's proposal. There was no point in pretending otherwise. "Yes," I whispered. "Let's go back to the changing room."

At first we were kind of mechanical about it. Maybe each of us was trying to keep some kind of vow. He dropped the towel and I held his stiff cock in my hand, stroking it slowly up and down. He reached out and placed a finger in my wet slit, rolling the tip around in my juice and swabbing lightly at my clit. We stood there facing each other and handling each other's genitals for several minutes. I was extremely excited.

Finally, with a shrug, I said, "What the hell." I moved toward him, put my arms around his neck, and lifted myself up, wrapping my legs around his powerful thighs. I could feel his cock gazing me where I wanted it to be. He leaned back against the wall, his hands on the cheeks of my ass, pulling me against him. He humped his hips, trying to work his erection in, until it found its mark and penetrated me.

My mind was spinning with images of all the naked people walking around outside. The remembered visions were making me hotter than hell. I was thrashing around so vigorously that his cock popped out a couple of times and he had to work it back inside. "*Oooohhh,* you're one hell of a hot chick," Mike moaned, and I knew he was about to shoot inside me.

I felt the swellings of his cock as it pumped and pumped. A moment later, I joined him, pouring my own juices all over the curling hair of his crotch. I was wrapped around him so tight that I seemed to be tottering on the wire that separated pleasure from pain. We bumped and ground against each other until our mutual orgasm was finished. Then I took a long, deep breath and disentangled myself. "For a white boy, you ain't too bad," I said. He laughed. We both felt comfortable, relieved of all tension.

We returned to the little cubicle twice more that day, as mingling with a hundred naked strangers got us both excited all over again. When evening approached, we were sorry that the day was coming to a close. Driving back to where we had left my car, I felt like kissing Mike for giving me such a wonderful time. That didn't happen. I didn't feel guilty about what we had done, but I think I would have felt guilty about a kiss.

Willard never suspected a thing. I've stopped mentioning my voyeuristic interests to him. He doesn't understand, and I don't want to give him reason to wonder about the occasional Saturday I spend with my girlfriends. That's what I tell him I'm doing when I get together with Mike.

We go to that nudist camp as Mr. and Mrs. Smith pretty regularly, considering that we both have other relationships. The thrill we both get from seeing naked strangers hasn't worn off and isn't going to. Now, besides being partners in voyeurism, we've become good friends. Every time we go to the resort, we end up satisfying each other in the changing room, just like we did that first time.

3

BOTH WAYS

SAME-GENDER SEXUALITY HAS RECEIVED A GREAT deal of media attention lately. Some of this has resulted from the work of homosexual organizations demanding legal and social recognition for their lifestyle. As that recognition grows, members of the mainstream public find themselves becoming more curious than ever about the things same-sex couples do behind closed doors. This curiosity fuels the media fires, bringing additional publicity to the subject.

By now, almost everyone knows someone who prefers sex with those of his or her own gender. Perhaps as a result, people who are and have always been heterosexual find themselves fantasizing about homosexual experimentation. Some go so far as to act out these fantasies.

Having a same-gender sex experience does not necessarily mean that a person is homosexual. It does not even make that person bisexual. We won't try giving a name to a sexual orientation that results more from curiosity than desire. We will simply repeat, in this chapter, the stories told to us by two individuals.

Suzanne and Leonard both found erotic bliss in ongoing same-sex relationships. Each of them has had this experience with only one other person. Each remains in a conventional marriage. Each claims to prefer sex with members of the opposite gender.

Both find something about carnal contact with a same-gender partner that is unequalled in a permanent, mainstream relationship. Neither can explain why this is, and we won't make any attempt to do so, either. We feel it is enough for us to report on their activity and let you draw your own conclusions.

TENNIS COACH

Suzanne is a young-looking forty, probably because she is very active, jogging every day and playing tennis several times a week. She is five feet eight inches tall and weighs about 135 pounds. Her dark brown hair is cut short and falls in natural curls around her head. Her pale blue eyes are unaccented by makeup. Although her body is athletic, she is unmistakably feminine, with a classic hourglass figure. She works a few hours a week as a Web site designer, unashamed to admit that she takes the rest of the time for herself.

My husband, Charles, makes plenty of money, so I don't really have to work at all. I just do it for self-respect, I suppose. He's the CEO of a company whose name you would recognize, so I'm not going to tell you which one. His work keeps him away from home quite a bit. I've got to take care of myself.

Maybe that's why I decided to get really good at tennis. I've been playing ever since high school, but I never took it very seriously until a few years ago. Then I made up my mind to improve my game. We belong to a country club with very nice courts and a wonderful tennis pro named Barbara, who gives lessons and organizes tournaments for the members.

Everybody knows Barbara's a lesbian, but nobody really gives a hoot. Who she sleeps with is her business. All that matters around here is that she's a hell of a tennis coach. When she was younger, she played on the pro circuit and was even rated in the top hundred for a couple of years. Now she's in her late thirties. Too old to compete, but young enough to instruct.

When I decided to work on my game, I spoke with her and arranged to take three one-hour lessons per week. At first she treated me like a beginner, going over grips and strokes as though I'd never held a racket in my hand before. After a few lessons, she started working on my serve. She would demonstrate the proper form and then have me try to repeat her movements.

When I watched her toss the ball in the air and raise her racket arm for the swing, I couldn't help but admire her shape. She was a very attractive woman. There wasn't an ounce of fat on her. Her slim body was muscular, yet at the same time there seemed to be a softness to her. When her shirt was wet with perspiration, I could see the dark circles of her nipples hard against it. Something about that sight appealed to me, although I didn't know why. And her eyes. She has the most startling blue eyes I've ever seen. They positively gleam, like with some kind of inner light.

I really admired her. A few times, when I watched her play with someone else, I found myself attracted to her in a strange way. At the time, I thought that what appealed to me was her enthusiasm for the sport. It was a great part of her teaching method, too. She would practically bubble over, telling me how much I improved with each session. I found myself looking forward to the lessons with great anticipation, not realizing at first that I was really looking forward to being with Barbara.

When I was working on my serve, or my return, or my ground strokes, she'd stand right behind me. Lightly, she'd place her hands on my shoulders or hips, turning me a little bit this way or that, to show me the proper position for the most effective shots. Once she even patted me on the fanny, telling me to pull my muscles in.

Each time she touched me, I felt a little spot of heat. It started where her fingertips made contact and seemed to work its way through my body. I began to crave her touch. I deliberately made myself slow to learn so she'd have reason to touch and correct me again. Something deep inside me wanted to stand behind her and touch her shoulders and hips and fanny the way she was touching mine.

We were becoming friendly, but I sensed that there was more to all this than friendship. Many times, I caught her looking at me in a way that I found very disconcerting. An attraction was developing, although I didn't understand that yet.

One afternoon I was trying to hit a power serve, when I pulled a muscle in my shoulder. It hurt so much that hot tears came to my eyes. I tried fighting them back, but Barbara noticed at once. She felt my shoulder, probing gently with her fingertips. When she found the spot that was most sensitive, she said, "There it is. You'll be okay in a couple of days, but I think we'd better stop for now." In spite of the pain, I was disappointed to be ending our session prematurely.

"Tell you what," she added. "Why don't you come to my office and I'll give you a massage. Maybe I can relieve some of the tension in that shoulder."

I was glad for the opportunity of spending a few more minutes with her. Truthfully, I thought I'd sit on a chair while she worked on my shoulder through the material of my tennis shirt. But when we got to her office, the first thing I saw was a massage table set up in the middle of the room.

"Take off your clothes and lie facedown on the table," she said. "I'll give you the works."

It usually seems perfectly natural to remove my clothing in front of other women. I do it all the time in the club's locker room. But something about this situation was filling me with a nervous excitement. Maybe it was because I knew she was a lesbian, or maybe it was because of the feelings I was already starting to develop for her.

When I hesitated, she said, casually, "I have to step out for a moment. I'll be right back." She closed the door behind her, leaving me alone with my doubts. I just shrugged and stripped down to my bra and panties. There was a folded sheet at the foot of the massage table. Lying facedown, I covered myself with it.

A few seconds later, Barbara returned. "Okay," she said, taking a bottle of oil from a shelf and pouring some onto the palms of her hands. She drew the sheet off to expose my back. "You can leave the panties on if you want to," she said. "But those bra straps are going to get in the way. Of course, if you're more comfortable . . ."

I reached back and unhooked the bra, managing to slip out of it without lifting myself too high off the table or revealing my naked breasts. I felt silly to be working so hard at staying covered, but something about the situation made me feel awkward. "Okay," I said. "I'm ready."

She moved around to the head of the table and began working on my shoulder. Her movements were very practiced and professional. As she stroked and kneaded, I could feel some of the pain and stiffness slipping away. I closed my eyes and allowed myself to be lulled by the comfort of her touch and the hand-warmed oil she was spreading over my skin.

After a while, she said, "We don't want to overdo that shoulder all at once. I'll work on your legs and low back and then return to it." She seemed to know exactly what she was doing. As she ran her hands up from my ankles to my mid-thighs and back again, I felt my nervousness leaving. It felt so good that it put me in a state of relaxed comfort.

Each stroke seemed to bring her hands gliding higher up my legs, closer and closer to my buttocks, which were still covered by my panties. I could feel her fingertips grazing the material as she ended the upstroke with a swooping circle that began the downstroke again. "You know," she said in a soft voice. "It really would be better without the panties."

I realized she was right. But it would be difficult for me to take them off without sitting up and revealing myself. For some strange reason, I was still trying to avoid that. Lying facedown on the table,

I reached back and tried working the panties down over my hips. It made my shoulder hurt again and I gasped involuntarily.

Sensing my difficulty, Barbara took the waistband of the panties in her fingers and began drawing them downward. "Can I help you with these?" she asked gently. I was trembling so hard inside that I couldn't even answer. To feel her stripping me of the last scrap of cloth that covered my nakedness was terrifyingly arousing. She tugged at them slowly, moving them lower and lower on my buttocks and then smoothly over my thighs. At some level, I knew that this was affecting her as much as it was me, maybe even more. In a moment, I was totally nude.

Now, when her hands smoothed the warm oil over my legs, the stroke did not stop until she had cupped and kneaded my buttocks. Sometimes she used both hands on one, twisting and squeezing the muscles. Sometimes she held one in each hand, lightly cupping and pressing against them. It felt so good I could have screamed. I didn't, of course, but I think I might have moaned a little.

As she stroked the cheeks of my bottom, she spread them slightly apart, her fingertips straying just to the edge of the valley between. Then she dipped directly into the crack of my backside, swabbing with the tip of an oiled finger. I sighed. Probably, that's what encouraged her. I just couldn't help it.

Lightly, almost by accident, her finger moved a little lower, dabbing almost imperceptibly at the lips of my vulva. It only stayed for a fraction of a second, not giving me a chance to protest or object. Not that I would have. I was too far gone. I'm not sure, but I think I might have raised my hips to give her easier access, to show her that I was willing to be touched that way.

I couldn't remember the last time I felt such excitement. Voices in my head were shouting, "No," "Yes," "No," "Yes," like the conscience of a confused schoolgirl. She stopped making any pretense now and cupped my vagina with her entire hand, running her fingers up and down the lips. She was seeking the swollen button of my clit, which I knew was standing out prominently from its little pink tent.

"You're very wet," she whispered. "Do you like what I'm doing?"

For a moment I was silent. Dare I say it? "Yes," I murmured at last. "Please don't stop."

I guess those words were what she was waiting to hear. All inhibitions were gone. She now had my permission. She inserted one stiff finger all the way inside my vagina and began twisting it as she worked it in and out. "Do you like this?" she asked.

"Yes," I said.

Then she gently squeezed the lips together and softly pinched them with her fingertips. "And this?"

She obviously enjoyed hearing me admit to the pleasure she was giving me. "Yes," I moaned. "I love that. Please do me more." I spread my legs wide, making it easier for her to stroke and fondle me. She kept it up for a while and then whispered, "Why don't you turn over."

Any embarrassment I might have felt was completely overpowered by the passion her touch was inspiring. I rolled quickly over onto my back. When I did, I saw that she had removed her shirt and bra. Her breasts were small and pointy, with dark pink nipples that stood out hard and erect. I could feel my heart beating.

I didn't know what to do. Barbara took my hands in hers and kissed them lightly. Then she placed them on her breasts. I had never touched another woman's breasts before. The feeling was incredible. Her nipples were pressed against the palms of my hands and I was free to explore her curves. Each stroke of my curious fingers brought a gasp of pleasure from her lips.

While I felt her breasts, she went back to touching my vagina. I threw my thighs as far apart as they could go, conscious that the pink membranes of my sex were completely visible to her. She petted them lightly and then bent forward to place her lips against my curling pubic hair. She inhaled sensuously and began lapping with her tongue at the wetness between my legs. She took my clit between her lips and sucked gently on it, rolling the tip of her tongue across its surface while her lips nibbled.

Carefully, methodically, she performed oral sex on me as no one ever had before. It was as though she knew instinctively what places were craving her touch, what contacts would please me most. Sometimes she just dabbled lightly at the outer lips with the tip of her tongue. Sometimes she plunged her entire tongue deep inside me, using it like a penis, but so much more tender and loving.

Without any preamble, I started to climax. As I moaned and groaned in the ecstasy of sexual release, she continued licking and sucking me, each shudder of orgasm making me more sensitive to her hungry mouthings. Just when I didn't think I could stand any more, I felt my excitement beginning to rise again.

For a moment, her lips abandoned me. I opened my eyes and tried to focus. There she was, frantically removing her shorts and panties. Then she was on the table with me, her knees on either side of my head, her vagina poised above my mouth. I stared at the loveliness of her. She was like a pink orchid.

When she started licking me again, I found myself lifting my head to bring my mouth in contact with her vulva. I couldn't believe how spicy and fragrant it was, how much the flavor of it was turning me on. A fire seemed to be raging in my chest. In a flash, I realized that this was something I had always imagined doing, always wanted to do. I applied myself to giving her pleasure as she had given and was giving me again.

Barbara lowered her hips so I could rest my head back on the table. She ground her pelvis around in circles, allowing my mouth to find every part of her. Her vagina seduced my lips, the way her lips had seduced my vagina. The scent and taste of her was magical, like a witch's elixir designed to inflame and arouse.

As soon as I sensed a change in the flavor of her juices, I realized that she was approaching orgasm. Knowing that I was giving it to her with my mouth, that I was bringing her the same glory she had brought to me, aroused me even further. As she started to come, I came again, with her. Honest to goodness, it was the first simultaneous orgasm I ever had with anyone. It was so intense, it felt like I had never come before.

The rest of the afternoon is a blur. I don't remember getting dressed or how we parted. I don't remember what we said to each other, or if either of us said anything at all. I just know that I went home in a daze, glad that Charles was out of town. I would not have been able to face him that night.

By the next day, when he got home, I had plenty of time to think it over. My afternoon with Barbara was the most wonderful sexual experience I ever had. It was my intention to have more experiences like it, if she was willing.

Of course, she was. At the end of my next tennis lesson, she casually asked, "Want to come back to my office?" I'm sure she knew what the answer would be. The second time was even better than the first.

Now, making love with Barbara has become a kind of ritual that we practice after each lesson. It's more sex than I have with Charles. And better, too. I don't know whether I should classify myself as "bi" or whether this is just something I have with Barbara. I don't really care. I know I'm still a heterosexual woman. I like having a husband. I like being married. But the sex I have with my female lover is the best I can even imagine.

PAY THE PRICE

Leonard is thirty-five with a compact, wiry body that seems to go with his dark, close-cropped curly hair and flashing black eyes. As he speaks, he keeps glancing around the room, as though worried that he will be seen and overheard. He makes a living washing windows on high-rise office buildings, bound to the sheer walls by nothing more than a leather safety strap, with its center fastened to his waist and its ends hooked onto cleats set in the concrete. He says the work appeals to the daredevil in him.

Look, I'm a happily married man, and if word of this ever got back to my wife my life would be absolutely ruined. So I really don't know why I'm telling you about it. I've never told anyone. No one else. Get it? I guess I'm hoping for some understanding from you. You must hear all kinds of stories. Maybe this won't be as much of a shock to you as it would be to just about anybody who knows me.

I've been married about six years. Before that, I was a real pussy chaser. Get it? I mean I would do anything for a hot piece of ass. Anything! I'd lie through my teeth if I had to. You know, tell 'em I loved 'em; tell 'em I needed sympathy; tell 'em I was in the CIA; tell 'em I was an escaped prisoner of war. Anything! Whatever it took. I'd pay for it, beg for it, work for it. Anything!

So one day—this was before I was married—I'm sitting in a bar having a beer, when this real good-looking chick comes up and sits down next to me. "I'm Lily," she says. "Wanna buy me a drink?" Oh, I can smell pussy a mile away, and this one is hot. So I go for it.

"Sure, I'll buy you a drink," I tell her. "What'll you have?" We sit there for a while, drinking and bullshitting, until I think the time is right. I figure this one is ripe for the direct approach. Get it? So I say, "How 'bout let's go someplace where we can have a little fun?"

She grins. "I was thinking the same thing," she says. "My apartment is only about a block from here. Come on back there with me, and I'll give you one hell of a fuck."

I can't believe what I'm hearing. I mean, this is really too good to be true. I'm off my bar stool and on my feet in about a tenth of a second. Then she says, "There's just one thing, though."

"Yeah?" I ask. "What's that?"

"My boyfriend," she says, calm as can be. "He's up there at the apartment. He won't mind if I fuck you, but he's gonna want to watch."

Sounded kinky to me, but what the hell. I told you I'd do anything for a piece of ass. The idea of fucking in front of an audience was a hot little twist. Get it? "No problem," I answer, slipping my arm around her waist.

"Oh, and there's one other thing," she adds.

"Yeah?" I ask, already propelling her toward the door. "What else?"

Just as we were hitting the street, she says, "He's going to want you to jerk him off first."

Now, that stopped me. Maybe I wasn't hearing it right. "He's going to want who to jerk him off?" I ask.

"You," she says. "After all, if he's going to let you fuck his girlfriend, that's the least you can do. What's the big deal?"

The way she put it made some kind of sense. What the hell, I told you I'd do anything for a fuck. So what if I gave the dude a handjob, as long as I got to screw her afterwards. "Okay," I say. "I'm down for it. Now, tell me, is there anything else I need to know before we go up there."

"No," she says. "That's all for now." And off we go.

Her place is up two flights in a building on the next street. When we get to her door, she starts slipping a key in the lock. Suddenly it opens from the inside, and this guy is standing there.

He's a good six feet tall, with shoulder-length blond hair and muscles like Hercules. His chest looks powerful and his hands are huge. Just for a minute, I wonder whether she brought me up here to get rolled and maybe killed. But the dude has a pretty face, and his voice is soft as velvet as he says, "Hi, there, I'm Brad."

"Hey, Brad," I say in greeting. My eyes are looking him over, wondering what it's going to be like to jerk him off. I've never done anything with a guy before; never wanted to. I still didn't want to, but I was willing to pay the price for a crack at his girlfriend. Get it? I don't mind telling you, I was nervous.

I had no idea how to get this thing started, but Lily saved me the trouble. "Take off your pants, Brad," she says. "My friend here . . . uh . . ." She stammers a bit, because I never did tell her my name.

"Leonard," I prompt.

"Yeah," she continues, as if nothing happened. "Yeah, Leonard here is going to give you a handjob. Then he's going to fuck me while you watch. Is that okay?"

"Yesss," Brad sort of hisses. I can see by the way his big chest is starting to heave that he is real excited. Without another word, he drops his pants and steps out of them. He isn't wearing any underwear, and his hard-on just pops out, pointing straight ahead.

I always thought I had a pretty big cock, but I never saw anything like this one before. The thing is gigantic. At least ten or eleven inches long, and as big around as my wrist. I gotta tell you, I'm thinking of backing out. I mean this is so weird. Here I am, supreme pussy king, getting ready to stroke another guy's dick. What the fuck was I doing?

But then Lily starts a slow strip. First her skirt, then her blouse. I stare at her in bra and panties, looking at her big tits swelling against the cups and seeing the shadow of her bush against the crotch of her drawers. Now I know I'm going through with it. Get it? Still looking at her, I reach out and take Brad's huge cock in my hand. He starts backing up slowly until he's sitting on a couch. I just kind of follow him.

By now, Lily is totally naked, and I'm staring at her, wide-eyed. I'm telling you, she has one hot body. "I'm not going anyplace," she says in a very husky voice. "You go ahead and pay attention to Brad's handjob. I'll be here when you're ready for me."

Well, I've done plenty of jerking off, so I was no stranger to handling a cock. Except this one wasn't mine. I know a few tricks to make it feel better when I'm jerking off, but I had no intention of using them on him. If this was a price I have to pay for a shot at Lily's pussy, I'm going to pay it as quick as I can and get what I came for.

So I start pumping that thing up and down for all I'm worth. It's big and fat and seems to get longer and thicker the more I handle it. Brad is leaning back against the cushions of the couch, making little noises with each movement of my hand. "Oh, yeah," he mumbles. "Oh, hold my balls, too. Please hold my balls."

I wasn't sure that was part of the deal, but what the hell. The quicker I get him off the sooner I get my cock into Lily. So I use my free hand to roll his balls around while I keep jerking up and down on his cock. It made a difference. I could see it. His hips lift up and move around in circles before slamming his ass back down against the couch.

Finally he lets out a kind of strangled cry, and his cock begins to spurt. I see the thick rolls of cum shooting out and flying in arcs across the room to land on the carpet. I just keep jerking and jerking until the last drop of it is out and his big dick starts to shrivel.

Then I turn to Lily. She's on her hands and knees on the floor, with her smooth white ass pointed up at me. "Come on," she whispers. "Fuck me like a dog."

I don't even bother to get undressed. I'm already hard as a rock and don't want to wait another minute. I just open my belt, push my pants and briefs down around my ankles, and drop to my knees behind her. Within a second, I have my cock in her pussy and I'm grinding away like mad. I was vaguely conscious that Brad was watching me fuck his girlfriend, but nothing really mattered except getting my rocks off. And I did, in just a minute or two.

When I get up and put my pants on again, Lily, still naked, hands me a piece of paper with her number written on it. "Call me," she says, "if you ever want to fuck me again." I stuffed it in my pocket and left.

I did call her, about a week later. She recognized my voice as soon as I said two words and invited me up for another fuck. I wondered if I was going to have to jerk the boyfriend off again, but I didn't ask. If I had to, it would be worth it for another piece of her pussy.

She surprises me, though, because when I get there and she opens the door for me, she says, "This time Brad wants a little more. Before you get to fuck me, you've got to fuck him in the ass. Is that okay?"

Now, here's the part I still find weird. I said it was okay. Even while I was saying it, I realized that as much as I wanted to knock off another piece of Lily, the idea of putting my cock up that guy's ass was appealing to me, too. I think I would have been willing even if she wasn't going to be waiting for a hot fuck afterwards. As I'm nodding dumbly, Lily hands me a condom.

Brad, who must have been listening from the other room, comes in immediately. He's completely naked, his huge cock sticking out like a pole in front of him. He stands facing the couch and bends over, showing me his open ass. I can see that he greased himself up with Vaseline or something in preparation.

Without any warm-up, I drop my pants and roll the rubber over my swollen dick. Then I move into position behind him, ramming my cock against the tight puckered opening of his asshole. I was hurting him and I knew it. For some strange reason, that was turning me on. He reaches back between his legs, takes my cock in his hand, and guides it into the opening, moving his body in a way that spreads the lips of his asshole and sucks me right in. I jam it forward, driving all the way to the hilt, hoping to hurt him good. He lets out a muffled moan and then starts stroking my balls.

I can't fucking believe how fucking good this feels. His ass is tighter than any pussy I've ever been in. His body is so muscular that the contractions of his asshole seem to be grabbing hold of my cock and milking it the way no woman ever did. He's groaning and moaning like he's getting ready to come, and I suddenly realize that if I don't pull out of him, I'm gonna come too. I don't know whether I tried and the tightness of his ass just held on to me, or whether I didn't really make an effort. The next thing I know, I'm shooting my load with my cock buried inside the guy.

I seemed to go away for a while, traveling to some hidden place inside myself. When I came back, I realized that Lily was sitting on the couch, naked, with her legs spread, rubbing her pussy while she watched me fucking her boyfriend. I was embarrassed and even ashamed that I got off, but she didn't seem to think there was anything wrong with it.

When my cock pops out of Brad, she reaches for me and pulls me toward her, slipping the wet condom off my prick and dropping it into an ashtray on the end table. With her hands and her mouth, she gets me hard again in just a few minutes. Then, pushing me into a sitting position on the couch, she gets into my lap, works my cock into her pussy, and rides me until I come again. And she comes with me.

"Pretty hot," was all she said when it was all over.

The next time I call her, I'm not sure whether I'm looking forward more to fucking Lily or Brad. This time, she wants to watch him give me a blowjob. The time after that, she wants to see me give him one. Pretty soon, him and I are doing everything two men can do to each other. I'm coming in his mouth. He's coming in mine. I'm laying on my back with my legs in the air while he mounts me and puts his cock up my ass.

Sometimes I fuck Lily afterwards. Sometimes I'm too worn out from my sex with Brad to bother with her. Finally we reach the point where I go to see him when she isn't even around.

Now get this straight: I never lost my interest in women. In between sessions with Brad, I'm still picking up every hot chick I can find. Still the pussy bandit. Get it?

Once, a couple of days after a session with Brad, I met a hot piece of ass in a laundry and ended up bringing her to my place for a night of sweet, sweet fucking. After a couple of months, we got married. It's a good marriage, too.

But I haven't stopped seeing Brad. I still get together with him every month or so. Most of the time, Lily isn't there. Even when she is, she usually stays in another room to give Brad and I some privacy. I have great sex with my wife, but nothing—I tell you, nothing—is as good as getting my cock into Brad's tight little ass or feeling him getting into mine. My wife can't give me what Brad gives me. Get it? No fucking way.

4
FOUNTAIN OF YOUTH

IN THE EIGHTH CENTURY, ALCHEMIST ABOU MOUSSAH Djafar wrote a series of classic works about the elixir vitae, a substance that would make a person live forever and maintain eternal youth. Djafar, known to history as "Geber," was not the first to search for the water of life. Neither he nor those who came before or after him ever found it.

In the sixteenth century, Spanish explorer Juan Ponce de León thought he would discover the fountain of youth in a place now known as Florida, U.S.A. From this mythical geyser would freely flow the tonic that could bestow youth everlasting on those who imbibed it. All Ponce de León got for his trouble was a poisoned arrow in the stomach at the age of sixty-one. It stopped him from getting any older.

Mortality is a fearsome concept, perhaps because of its inevitability and our uncertainty about what will follow death. For some people, the prospect of getting old is even more frightening than that of shuffling off the mortal coil. They fear the disabilities that tend to come with advancing years, the sexual disabilities in particular. Since reproduction of the species is the most important function of any living creature, the inability to procreate is perceived by many as a dramatic sign of uselessness. Although the power to create offspring usually leaves long before the ability to go through the reproductive motions, loss of sexual potency is terrifying evidence of the approaching end of life.

The people whose stories are told in this chapter began to feel the weight of their years while still in middle age. Each discovered it by noticing that the sexual excitement had gone out of marriage. In their own minds, they managed to restore their disappearing youth by having secret sexual affairs with younger persons.

POOL SERVICE

Monica is forty-six and makes no attempt to hide it. Gray hair mingles freely with black to give her shoulder-length coif a salt-and-pepper look. Her green eyes are surrounded by tiny laugh lines, as is her full-lipped mouth. But her tall, slender figure makes her attractive in spite of her age. Her breasts are full, nearly half a century of fighting gravity giving them only the slightest hint of sag. Her voice is a bit husky, with a sexy tone that somehow manages to combine the sounds of wisdom and experience.

I guess I'm what used to be called a housewife. It's always been that way. My husband, Frederick, brings home the bacon and I take care of all our domestic needs. Our two children are grown, so there's a lot less for me to do now, but I still consider homemaking to be a more-or-less full-time job. I don't mind it at all, even though it might not be politically correct for me to say that.

I like to cook and I take pride in having Frederick's dinner waiting on the table when he gets home in the evening. I don't mind doing the laundry. I even like ironing his shirts. He doesn't take me for granted. We see our life as a partnership with division of labor.

A few years ago, I started to have a horrible sinking feeling. It had nothing to do with my household chores. Just with my age. I was hitting my mid-forties and I didn't like it. As all young people do, I spent the first part of my life believing I was immortal. Eventually, I came to accept the idea that life is only temporary, but I hate the idea of being old.

Oh, some of the women I know dye their hair, or use that Retin stuff to make the wrinkles go away, or even get plastic surgery. But that really doesn't make them any younger. To me, it doesn't even make them look younger. I knew I'd have to learn to live with my advancing years. It was starting to get depressing.

Especially on every second Thursday, when Brett came to clean our pool. When he started, I don't think he was more than twenty and the perfect picture of young manhood. He's tall and muscular and blond, with broad shoulders and legs like marble columns. He'd stand at the edge of the pool, wielding a long-handled brush and wearing nothing more than a brief pair of cutoff jeans. I couldn't help watching him through the window, admiring his masculine beauty. The more I looked, the older I felt, but I was fascinated. I just couldn't look at him enough.

Honestly, I don't think there was anything erotic about my thoughts. It brought back memories of when I, too, was young, and vital, and in my sexual prime. Aaaaahhh, if only I could turn back the hands of time.

I don't believe it's as much of a problem for men. They seem to get more distinguished-looking as we start looking older. Sometimes Frederick stands in front of the mirror and says he looks better than he ever did in his life. You know, I'm pretty sure he's right.

I don't think I had any of this on my mind as I lay out on the pool deck one Wednesday afternoon. The hedges around our yard are high enough to block all view from the outside, and Brett wasn't due to come service the pool until the following day. It was warm, not a cloud in the sky, and I wanted to work on my tan. So I slipped out of my bathing suit and lay nude on a lounge chair alongside the pool. I think I fell asleep.

Suddenly I awoke with a start. Even before I opened my eyes,

I had the feeling that someone was watching me. I squinted into the sun, and sure enough, there was Brett. He was standing there in his cut-offs, his mouth slightly open, his eyes wide. He was staring at me, but not in an insolent way. When he saw that I was awake and looking at him, he turned away and grinned sheepishly.

"I'm sorry," he said. "I didn't mean to sneak up on you. I've got to go out of town tomorrow and thought I'd do your pool a day early." Then he blurted, "I didn't mean to gawk, but, my God, you really are beautiful."

His words made me remember, for the first time, that I was totally naked. I reached for my bathing suit, which I had placed on the ground next to the lounge chair, but it was gone. From the corner of my eye, I saw it floating on the surface of the water. The wind must have carried it into the pool. My towel was draped over the diving board, where I had left it.

I felt my face reddening. Here I was totally exposed to this young man's gaze. I wanted to cover my breasts and groin to block his view, but I didn't have enough hands. Besides, the very idea seemed so undignified. Mustering all the cold deliberation I could, I said, "Would you mind handing me my towel."

Brett obeyed, but rather slowly, I thought. As he stepped to the board and returned to my lounge, his eyes remained riveted to my naked body. I could feel myself becoming physically aroused by his appreciative stare. My nipples hardened, and it was too warm a day to blame it on a cold breeze.

As he passed the towel to me, Brett murmured, almost under his breath, "What a shame to cover up such a beautiful body."

"I don't feel that way," I responded, holding the towel in my hand but not covering myself with it. "It might have been beautiful at one time, but not anymore."

"Oh, I wouldn't say that," he said, taking a step towards me. There was a question in his eyes, and I suppose I answered it with mine. A moment later, he was on his knees beside the lounge chair, pressing his lips against my naked belly. It was a turning point. I could have stopped it right there and then with a word or a gesture. But I didn't. Instead, I sighed.

Apparently, that was all the encouragement he was waiting for. His lips nibbled and kissed their way up to my breasts and he began sucking gently on my nipples. From that moment on, I was completely in his power. My arms snaked around his neck to pull him against me. His lips found mine and we kissed long and deep, as I had not done since my twenties. It was strange yet wonderful.

An instant later, he was all over me. His hands, his mouth, his arms were touching me everywhere. I felt I was reliving my youth. I was carried away on a tide of passion. I reached for him, running my fingertips over his chest and back and shoulders, knowing that every move I made drove him to take further liberties.

Suddenly his head was between my legs and his mouth was kissing and nibbling my inner thighs and my most private spot. Frederick hadn't made love to me this way in years. It was wonderful. I was experiencing sensations that only the young can experience.

Brett picked me up in his powerful arms and carried me into the pool. I don't know how, but he managed to shed his shorts somewhere along the way. I could feel his manhood hard and strong against me as he lowered us both into the sun-warmed water. I wanted to feel it in my hand and reached down for him. It seemed so huge and mighty, proclaiming its youthful power with a series of throbbing pulsations.

He was murmuring a steady stream of erotic narrations, some much dirtier than I was accustomed to hearing. "Yeah," he whispered. "I want to fuck that gorgeous body of yours. I want my cock inside your hot pussy. I want to fill you with cum."

I was hypnotized, as much by his words as by his touch. I wrapped my legs around his and used my hand to guide his erection inside me. I was distinctly aware of the entry beginning, his massive thickness spreading my tissues and seeming to force its way in. He worked his hips, driving deeper and deeper. It felt like there was no end to the length of him. At last, I felt the bones of his pelvis against my body and I knew that he was in as far as he could possibly be.

We began moving together, grinding back and forth in the age-old rhythm of sex. My eyes were tightly shut, as if I wanted to concentrate all my attention on this wonderful sensation, on the sliding, ramming, jamming, twisting plunges. I could feel the water lapping gently at my breasts, along with his tongue, which kept playing over the sensitive erect little mounds of my nipples.

What a glorifying experience. The water. The powerful arms that held me against him. The iron thighs that supported our buoyant weight. And the penis driving into me as if I were a tight young virgin.

"I'm going to come in you," he blurted. "Oh, I'm going to come in you."

His words were the final straw. If I had any restraint left, it faded at that moment. I practically screamed. "Oh, yes, come in me. I'm going to come, too." Then it began.

I usually have orgasms when making love with Frederick, but I could not remember anything as powerful or intense as this one. In the arms of this young man, I was being brought to the absolute pinnacle of ecstasy. I could feel his youthful exuberance discharging inside me, pumping, rocketing, filling me with his essence. I almost drowned in a maelstrom of feeling.

Moments later, I was lying on the lounge chair again, Brett by my side, both of us gasping for breath. "My God," he said. "You are a fantastic woman. I've always had fantasies about making love to you, and I can't believe it actually happened. More than that, I can't believe how good it was. I've been wasting my time until now with Valley girls and spoiled brats. Now I know what a real woman is."

His words flattered me, perhaps more than they should have. Suddenly I didn't feel like an aging woman. Mature, yes, but my maturity made me an object of desire. For the first time in years, I was feeling good about myself. I wasn't old. I was vintage.

I hated to see Brett leave and wondered whether it would ever happen again. Well, it has. Almost every time he comes to service the pool. Frederick doesn't suspect a thing and would never guess it in a million years. I'm not even sure whether he realizes that his wife is happier and has become a better lover to him. But I know I am. And I think I owe it all to my affair with Brett.

HERBAL TREATMENT

Jason just turned fifty-one. Although his body is still firm and trim, his face shows his years. There are dark circles around his hazel eyes and his cheeks are a bit jowly. He darkens his almost gray hair with something he buys in the drugstore, but cannot cover the fact that it is thinning and somewhat limp. He says that he used to be six feet tall; however, according to his last physical, he's lost an inch. As an optometrist managing a franchised lens establishment, he wears glasses in stylish frames.

I'm not getting old, but let's face it, I'm certainly getting older. I can't eat the way I used to anymore, unless I'm willing to put up with heartburn. I have to prescribe stronger glasses for myself every twelve or fourteen months. I never expected to be taking ginkgo extract to prevent memory loss, but now I take it every day. Unless I forget.

That's not the only herbal I'm taking, either. When my wife and I were younger, we were a couple of horn dogs. Just couldn't get enough sex. It seemed like I was always fighting an erection. She was always ready to take me on. We've been married for twenty-three years. The first ten were a never-ending orgy. Now we hardly ever have sex.

It started maybe six or seven years ago. I was no longer struggling to keep my erection down. Sometimes I had to work at getting it up. It wasn't too bad at first, because my wife was still interested enough in sex to do what was necessary to get me hard. Then it started to mean less and less to her, and she was no longer willing to work at it.

It's a body-mind thing. My mind still wanted it like crazy. Sometimes I'd want a piece so badly that I'd get frustrated as hell. My body simply was not willing to oblige. At least not without help, and I wasn't getting any from her. I tried a couple of herbal treatments, but without a willing partner the results were pretty dismal.

I found myself getting depressed, which was a new experience for me. I was always a pretty happy kind of guy. Oh, like anyone else, I might have an occasional bout of sadness or mild depression, but this was becoming chronic. Part of it was the frustration that came from not getting any sex. The other part was an overwhelming feeling that I was getting old.

There's a woman who works at the eyeglass center with me. Anita. She's about twenty years younger than I am. She first came to work for me a long time ago, when she was in optometry school. We were pretty friendly at the workplace. You know, flirting and kidding around and that sort of harmless stuff. But we never saw each other socially. I don't think we've ever met outside the store.

It's a little close behind the counters, and sometimes we'd brush against each other accidentally. Nothing was ever said about it. It didn't mean anything. Nothing at all. Then one day about three years ago, suddenly it did.

She was squeezing past me and the soft curve of her breast brushed up against my chest. The thing is, it gave me an erection. Well, maybe not a full-on erection, but the kind we used to call a semi-hard. Just for a moment, she seemed to glance down at it. Then she looked away.

I don't mind telling you, I was embarrassed. But that's not all I was feeling. I was feeling like a man again. Responding that way to a woman was something that hadn't happened to me for a while. It stayed on my mind all day. When I got home that night, I thought I'd be ready to make love to my wife. But somehow, nothing could bring back the feeling. Or the erection. Maybe if she had made a little effort it would have been different. But my wife really wasn't interested.

The next day, I deliberately looked for an opportunity to rub up against Anita, just to see if it would happen again. We were both behind the counter putting new frames in the showcase. This time, as she was bending over, I let my hand sweep casually across her bottom. I tried to make it seem like an accident, just a light grazing contact. It worked. Instantly. This time, I was as hard as a rock. I could feel my face flush with heat, when I realized that my turgidity would be obvious. I tried to turn away, but she looked back before I did.

"Why, Jason," she said, giggling. "Are you happy to see me, or is that a pistol in your pocket?"

I was so ashamed, I felt like a kid caught staring at the teacher. "I'm really sorry for my condition," I stammered. "I haven't had a problem like this in years."

She smiled. "Is everything all right at home?" she asked.

"Oh, yeah," I replied. "It's nothing like that. Everything is fine." Then I added in an almost inaudible whisper, "Everything except my sex life."

I was quite embarrassed, but although Anita is a generation younger than I, she didn't seem to be embarrassed at all. Must be that age gap everybody talks about.

"Really?" she said. "I never would have thought you had a problem like that. You're a very sexy man." Her words were pleasing to me. "I haven't had any sex since my divorce," she added. "So I can understand how you feel."

I didn't know what to say, so I just turned away and busied myself at the other end of the store. I tried to put our conversation out of my mind, but the erection persisted. At five, I locked the front door as usual and put the CLOSED sign in the window. The day's work wasn't done. We still had a few repairs to do in the back room before we would be able to leave.

We were sitting side by side at the bench, working on customers' glasses, when suddenly Anita leaned over and put her hand in my crotch. I felt myself spring to full erection. "I've been thinking about what you said earlier," she said in a soft, husky voice. "And about how big you looked inside your pants."

I just sat there paralyzed and shocked into silence.

"Are you really as big as you look?" she asked. I didn't know what to say. "Why don't you show me," she prompted.

As she spoke, she found the zipper of my fly. She ran her fingers up and down its length for a moment, then, slowly, she zipped it open. "Come on, now," she whispered playfully. "You show me yours and I'll show you mine."

I was beyond any kind of self-control. My muscles were all turned to jelly and my brain was completely scrambled. Anita led the way. Guiding me with her hands, she got me to my feet. Then she undid my belt and slipped my trousers and undershorts down my legs until they were twisted around my ankles. My penis had not been this stiff or hard in years. She took it in her hand and stroked it once or twice.

"You are every bit as big as I thought," she said. Then, turning her back to me, she said, "Unzip me. I want us both to be naked." Like a robot following commands, I unzipped the back of her dress and helped her step out of it. Seeing her in her underwear made me tremble with excitement.

When she turned to face me again, my eyes went to the rounded curves swelling over the tops of her lacy brassiere cups. She twisted a catch located between them and the bra fell open to reveal her pink-tipped breasts. I sighed involuntarily. She smiled as she slipped out of her sheer panties. I was mesmerized by the dark shadow of her pubic triangle. The hair was thick and curling.

Her hands began fumbling with the rest of my clothes, pulling and tugging until I was as naked as she. Then, with exaggerated slowness, she dropped to her knees in front of me and took my penis in her mouth. I had almost forgotten how good it feels to be completely engulfed by a woman's hot lips, to have her tongue working its way up and down and all around.

I bent slightly forward so that I could cup her firm young breasts in my hands. The nipples felt like two burning embers against my palms. As she sucked and licked me, she made little humming noises in her throat, creating vibrations that warmed me to my very soul. I couldn't remember the last time I was this hard, or the last time I had oral sex that felt this good.

After thoroughly wetting and mouthing my penis, Anita got up off her knees and leaned her naked body back against the workbench. Her legs were spread wide, inviting me toward her. I put one arm around her shoulders, and with the other hand I started to massage the thick bush of hair that surrounded her sex. As my fingers gently stroked through her curling pubes, I could feel liquid oozing from her vagina and the lips parting. My finger easily found its way inside the warmth of her. Her sexual moans were driving me wild.

Deeper and deeper my finger explored her warm lush vulva, while her hips rotated excitedly with my movements. I moved my finger up until I found her distended clitoris and fondled it gently. Removing my arm from her shoulders, I reached for one of her aroused nipples. I heard a gurgle of lust come from Anita's throat. Whatever I was doing to her, I was doing right. It felt wonderful to be able to bring such passion and excitement to a woman again. I was feeling stronger and more able than ever.

Anita reached out and held my penis, which was so hard now that it stood out straight in front of me and was practically touching her belly. Our bodies rotated, simulating the motion of intercourse, while she stroked me with her hand and my fingers moved freely inside her.

"You'd better slow down," she sighed, moving reluctantly away from my touch. "I feel like I'm going to come." I understood. My hard penis was also about to erupt, and I wanted to be inside her.

I moved my hand to her other breast, gently but firmly rolling and playing each nipple. As her moans became louder and louder, Anita's hand guided my penis between her legs, using its tip to part her oozing lips. Slowly I felt my erection slipping its way into her. Then with a sudden burst of power, she pushed her pelvis up and forward against me. I was buried deep inside her. She was so wet that I glided easily in and out of her.

I hadn't been inside a woman's vagina in a long time. I couldn't ever remember it being as good as this. The sexual heat of her vaginal channel completely surrounded me, elevating my sexual temperature to the boiling point. It felt as though her vulva was lined with a million fingers, all rubbing and stroking and massaging and petting my swollen erection as it plunged to her bottom.

I pulled slightly back to begin another stroke. The flesh of her vulva seemed to follow my retreating penis, unwilling to release its hold on me, aching to keep the contact, fearful of its loss. Then, when I reversed and moved in again, the folds of her inner vagina rolled back to welcome me, to wrap themselves around my shaft as it drove for her center. Each time I struck the knob of her cervix deep inside the darkness of her sex, she grunted a primal sound of satisfaction. I harmonized with her, adding my cries to hers.

I was aware that an orgasm was lurking at the base of my consciousness, gathering at the seat of my scrotum, swelling my testes screaming for release. I was losing control. I was going to explode. I wanted to wait for her, but I could not hold back any longer. Confessing the discharge with a growl, I began pumping into her, filling her with my essence, cascading the pent-up fluids that my frustration had stifled for all this time.

I continued to come and come and come, hoping that it would last long enough for Anita to join me. She seemed to take a special satisfaction in my orgasm, murmuring encouraging obscenities in my ear as I gushed into her. "Yes, fuck me deep," she moaned. "Fill me with cum. Don't hold anything back."

I kept driving in and out of her, my penis remaining hard long after my fluids were spent. At last, reaching between us, I began rubbing her clitoris with my finger as I continued moving my erection in and out. That seemed to be what she had been waiting for.

Almost immediately, I could hear the timbre of her voice changing, becoming throatier, almost bestial. She sounded like she was choking, as her body released its ecstasy in flowing waves. It went on for a long time, her vulva contracting around my penis as my finger kept her climax coming.

When it was all over, I at last went limp. Not just my sex organ, by my whole body suddenly felt as though all strength had left it. I slid down to the floor and rested. She joined me, rolling into my arms. For a long time, we were silent, each listening only to the sound of the other's breathing.

"My God," she whispered at last. "No one has ever made me come like that. You are an incredible lover." Her words brought me as much satisfaction as the orgasm had. I pulled her against me and kissed her on the mouth.

Anita and I have had an ongoing affair ever since. Sometimes I feel like I could make love to her every day. But I guess if I did, the wonder of it all would wear off. No, Anita is too smart for that. She sort of rations it. Somehow we manage to continue working together in a professional relationship until she lets me know that she wants another episode. Usually she does that by brushing up against me behind the counter and maybe touching my crotch the way she did that first time. Then we wait until closing and make love in the back room.

Nothing has changed at home, but I don't feel as old as I did before this began. In a strange way, my feelings for my wife have grown more tender. I think having Anita in my life is a good thing for me and for my marriage. It sure beats those herbal treatments.

5

GIVE ME MORE

IN THE 1880S, ENGLISH SCIENTISTS DISCOVERED THAT no two fingerprints were alike. They soon created the fingerprint identification system still in use by police departments around the world. Since then, no one has ever discovered a fingerprint on one person that was duplicated on the hand of another.

Sexual patterns are also unique, with no two persons having exactly the same tastes or desires. This is especially true in terms of frequency. Woody Allen illustrated the point in his film *Annie Hall*, in a split scene in which two partners in a relationship were talking to their therapists. The man complained that his girlfriend was frigid, because she didn't want to have sex more than two or three times a week. The woman called her boyfriend a sex fiend, saying that he was never satisfied, not even by having sex two or three times a week.

It may happen that the male partner wants more sex than the female, or that the female wants more sex than the male. Either way, it is unlikely that one person will want sex whenever the other does. This may require the partners to find some mutual accommodation, or it may lead one of them to seek sexual fulfillment outside the relationship.

That's what happened to Bo and Megan, the people whose stories are told in this chapter. Each of them is honest enough to recognize that the only reason for the infidelity is an interest in finding sexual release. Neither is honest with his or her mate, however. In both cases, the hunger that drives them and the means they have found for satisfying it remain secret.

TOPLESS BAR

At twenty-nine, Bo is a successful entrepreneur, although a person seeing him for the first time might not think so. He wears his long black hair in a ponytail that reaches to his mid back, and it has a greasy, unkempt look to it. His brown eyes are heavily lidded, as if he's been too long in a smoke-filled room. His jeans and sport shirt are none too clean and hang somewhat loosely on his thin frame. He is about five feet ten inches tall. Most of the time, his sallow face wears a bored expression, except when he talks about his sex life or his business.

I inherited this place from my father when he died two years ago. He had some dumb idea about having live jazz music on the weekends, as if that would bring in the crowds. It ended up costing him more than he was making. It was nothing more than a neighborhood bar until I took over.

For a while, I tried running it his way. But I got fed up with serving drinks to the local working men and just making ends meet. My wife used to help out, slinging beers on busy nights. We had been married about three years when my father passed away, and the idea of working together kind of appealed to both of us.

I'm really horny. I mean I've got an incredible sexual appetite. My wife likes plenty of sex, too, but she can't really keep up with me. When she worked here, we'd slip into the storage room a couple of times a night for a quickie. You know, she'd lift her dress. I'd stick it in. Wiff wham, thank you ma'am, and back to work. I liked it that way, but she seemed to be getting tired of it.

Besides, business really sucked. I decided I was going to have to do something about both problems. One, build up the business. And, two, find a way of satisfying my sex cravings. It wasn't a matter of quality. It wasn't a matter of variety. It was just a matter of quantity. I needed more fucking than my wife was willing or able to provide.

I don't exactly remember what gave me the idea of turning the place into a topless bar, but it was perfect. It would solve all my problems at once. There's a Navy base not all that far from here, and those sailors love titty bars. Most of them are kids, with nothing to spend their money on but having a good time. I knew that my wife wouldn't continue working here if we went topless. That was fine with me, because I decided to make fucking the boss part of every dancer's job description.

At first I was worried about getting the licensing. Then I found a real good lawyer. He had me going in no time. He told me that I would be in big trouble unless I made it clear that there was to be no hanky-panky between the girls and the customers. He never said anything about the owner, though.

As soon as I was legal, I started interviewing girls who wanted to be dancers. I'm still interviewing. Shit, it's the best part of the business.

At first I was surprised at how easy it was. I ran one little ad in the paper and ended up getting more girls than I could use in three lifetimes. I have to pay minimum wage—that's the law—but the girls know if they're good at shaking their booty in the customers' faces they'll make a bundle in tips.

I heard that some bar owners make the dancers split tips with the management, but I tell all the job applicants that they can keep everything they take in. Naturally, that makes me a more desirable employer and makes them more willing to tolerate my special requirements. About halfway through each interview, I say that I expect them to put out for me whenever I want it. Some of them walk away when they hear that. There are still plenty who want the job enough to accept my terms. I get more girls than I can use.

I remember the first one I interviewed. She calls herself Sasha. They all pick names like that, sexy names. Sasha still works here. When I told her about my tipping policy, her eyes lit up. When I got to the part about fucking me whenever I wanted, she just shrugged. "How about right now?" she asked.

I grinned. This was working out exactly the way I'd hoped. "Just a quick one," I said, standing up and unzipping my pants.

She dropped her drawers right on the spot. "How do you want it?" she asked. "Standing up? On the floor? In your chair?"

I told her the floor would be fine, and she stretched out without a minute's hesitation, her legs spread wide to show me her pussy. "Go ahead," she said, framing her manicured bush with her hands. "Put it right there."

I got down between her thighs and lowered myself onto her, letting my cock slide straight in. She made some little theatrical sounds in her throat to convince me that she was having a good time, but that didn't fool me. Anyway, I don't really care whether a girl has a good time or not. I just wanted to pop my nuts. A couple of quick strokes and I felt it coming. Then, boom, there it was. I kept going until I was done, and then got up and zipped my pants again.

"Well," she said. "Do I get the job?" Naturally, I hired her on the spot.

Since then, I got the interviews down to a routine. First, I ask the girl a few questions and check her ID to make sure she's old enough. Then I make her show me her tits. Since they dance in the teeniest bikini bottom imaginable, I am going to have to see them completely naked sooner or later, but there is something about making them show me the tits first that I especially enjoy.

I say it just that way, real rough. "Okay, now show me your tits!" Even some of the experienced girls get a little flustered when I put it like that. The ones who never worked before usually turn bright red. But, of course, if they are applying for jobs as topless dancers, they know in advance that they are going to have to undress.

I sit here watching coldly as they undo their buttons or zippers of whatever it is they have on. The girls who've had boob jobs usually don't wear bras. Their titties pop right out at me, standing straight up, like my dick. The customers love those big, perfect-shaped plastic boobs, but I prefer the natural ones, even if they sag a little.

My personal preference is when they have a bra on, because I love seeing those come off. Lots of the new bras hook in the front, but I like the ones that fasten in the back. I really dig watching those girls struggle to reach back and unhook them. Stretching that way seems to show the tits to best advantage.

I study the tits for a while, paying special attention to the nipples. You'd be amazed at how many different kinds of nipples there are. I love the puffy ones that look like little plums stuck on to the end of the titties. Sometimes, I might reach out and touch one, saying that I have to make sure it's real.

After a while, I say, "Well, you passed the first test. Now I'll have to see the rest of the bod. Take everything off." This always seems to be easier for them, I guess because the ice was already broke when they showed their tits. I'll still be sitting here, acting real businesslike while I watched the strip show.

When they are completely naked, I make them turn around real slow, so I can see every part of them. Sometimes, when their backs are to me, I make them bend over. It's a typical move a dancer makes, so it don't seem unusual for me to insist on seeing it. I like it because it spreads the ass cheeks and gives me a good look at the pussy.

At that point, I pretty much know whether she is the kind of girl I intend to hire. But there is still that one last test. I put them all to it, whether I plan on giving them the job or not. "You know," I say. "There are a lot of girls who want to work here. I can afford to be very choosy." I let this sink in for a minute, and then I add, "So it's got to be completely understood that any girl who works for me has to put out for me whenever I ask her to."

I wait another minute and then ask, "How do you feel about that?" Some get huffy. Those I tell to get lost. Some just say, no, they aren't that hungry for work. I tell them to get lost, too, but in a gentler way. Most of them act like they're thinking it over and end up saying that it's all right with them. Then comes the moment of truth, when I say I want a sample right then and there.

I always do it quick and rough, just to get myself off. I want them to know right from the start that I'm not interested in being a boyfriend or a lover. Just a fucker. I think most of them like it better that way, anyways. Lots of them already have boyfriends. They might end up letting their boyfriends know they are fucking the boss, or not. I didn't really give a shit.

After I fuck one of the applicants, I usually tell her that I have to think it over and will let her know in a day or two. That way I don't have to tell any of them to their faces that they aren't getting the job. At the end of a day's interviews, I think back and decide which ones were the best lays, and those are the ones I call.

When I opened with the topless format, business started booming right from the beginning. The money was absolutely rolling in. My wife wasn't exactly crazy about the idea of me running a topless bar, but when I brought home the buckage, she swallowed all her objections. It's still going strong.

The show begins at eleven in the morning and runs continually until closing time at two A.M. We rotate through twelve dancers a day. Usually, I take a couple of hours off to go home for dinner and knock off a quick one with my wife. The rest of the time, though, I rule my little palace. I decide what order the girls perform in and I pick the music they dance to.

Three or four times a day, I call one of them into my office in the back for a piece of ass. I don't have a preference for any particular dancer. They're just sex toys to me. I keep it strictly impersonal. I fuck them standing on my feet, bending them over the edge of my desk, sitting in my lap in my big swivel chair, or laying down on the floor. Sometimes, I just have them give me a blowjob. I take it wherever, whenever, and however I feel like it. Every day is filled with sex and money.

It's like having my own personal harem, a different woman anytime I feel like it. For the first time in my life, my sexual appetite is being truly satisfied. I'm happier than I ever was before.

I'm sure my wife suspects something, because I'm not constantly climbing all over her like I used to be. But she never asks. It's funny how a pocket full of money can ease a woman's mind and make her happy. The girls are making big bucks in tips, so they don't mind taking care of the boss. I'm getting all the pussy I can use, so I don't mind the long hours. My wife can buy anything her little heart desires, so she doesn't much care how I amuse myself at work. I'd say it works out pretty well for just about everyone.

AIRPORT HAIRDRESSER

Megan is twenty-eight but could easily pass for twenty. She is five-foot-seven, with a trim waist, a big bosom, and narrow girlish hips. Her flaming red hair is stylishly short, and her makeup is impeccable. Her lips are sensuously full, the result, she admits, of collagen injections. Her light brown eyes are carefully outlined in five or six different subtle hues of shadow, as though done by an expert cosmetician. In fact, that is her trade. Megan operates a hairdressing shop located at an international airport.

I do hair for both sexes, but very few of my customers are female. Women prefer to go to the same hairdresser all the time and are not likely to drop in for a haircut at the airport. Men tend to be less picky. Lots of them come in for a trim just because they have a few hours to kill between planes and don't know what else to do with themselves. Sometimes I give them a real surprise.

I've been living with my boyfriend, Kenneth, for almost seven years. We aren't married and haven't got any plans along those lines. I don't really think I'm marriage material. Forsaking all others till death do us part and all that stuff just isn't for me. One man will never be enough.

Kenneth is a good enough bed partner, but he just doesn't have the stamina to give me what I need sexually. Deep down, I don't believe any man alive would be able to do it. I need much more sex than most people do. Three or four times a day is just about enough to keep me satisfied. Even on weekends, Kenneth hasn't got that much in him.

I've always been that way. Even in high school, the other girls called me Megan-the-nymph. The guys all said that I was an easy lay. I know they talked about me in the locker room and all that stuff. They thought they were using me, but I was using them just as much. I need lots and lots of sex. The only way I've ever been able to get it is by having lots and lots of different men.

Kenneth doesn't know it, of course. It's a secret I'll always have to keep from him. If he did know, I'm sure it would fracture his precious male ego, and that would be the last I'd see of him. It's too bad men can't understand that, for a woman like me, there's a difference between sex and love. I can have sex with dozens of men and still love only one. It's kind of funny, because men understand that feeling when they have it. They just don't believe that a woman can be the same way they are.

If it wasn't for my business, I think I'd either end up walking the streets, or I'd live with total sexual frustration. Lucky for me I discovered a solution. Men who are worlds away from their homes pass through my salon between planes every day. I rarely see the same one twice. When I find one who appeals to me—and most men do—I flirt outrageously. Then I let him pursue me until I catch him.

The salon is small. Just one chair. Just me. I don't even have a waiting area. When I've got a customer, there's no room for anyone else. I do have a little back room, though. It's barely big enough for the bed I keep there. Supposedly, I have it for taking naps in the middle of the day. In reality, that's where I bring my men when I've let them succeed in seducing me.

There was an Italian guy here earlier today who was really surprised when he saw it. He was in his forties and rather distinguished-looking. You know, a little gray mixed in with his lustrous black hair. He was dressed to kill in that special way that affluent Italian men have.

He had been in the U.S. for a couple of days on business and was flying back to Italy, when he found himself with time to kill. I saw him giving me the eye through the window before coming in. He needed a haircut like a hole in the head. It was obvious he was there to make a pass.

He thought he was being cute and coy, flirting in that oily continental manner and all that stuff. While I cut his hair, he kept making double-meaning jokes in his cultured Italian accent. He called me *bella* and *bellissima*. From time to time, I caught him looking surreptitiously at his watch, trying to figure out whether there was enough time for him to really put the heavy make on me. I gathered he was getting ready to invite me to lunch or something, so I cut right to the chase.

"Look," I said. "How much time do you have before your flight? I've got something in the back you might be interested in."

He was a little confused by this. What could I possibly have to interest him? "About two hours," he answered hesitantly. Then he seemed to get nervous. "But, I . . ."

"Never mind the buts," I said. "Come with me." I locked the front door and led him into the back room. He stood there for a minute, just staring at the bed and blinking his eyes. "Stop wasting time," I said. With that I gave him a push. He wasn't expecting it and fell right onto the bed. He just lay there for a minute looking at me in a state of total confusion. Without a word, I started unbuttoning my blouse.

"*Mamma mia,*" he said. "This is a surprise. Do all American women approach foreign men this way?"

"I don't know about the rest," I answered. "But I do." I stripped my clothes off quickly and stood before him in my underwear. "Come on," I said. "What the hell are you waiting for? You said you've only got two hours."

He stood up at once and began getting undressed. "Have I stumbled into paradise?" he asked. "Can this really be happening?" His eyes were pasted to the satin material of my bra, to the spots where my hard nipples poked against it.

"Get naked," I said. "Then finish undressing me."

With that, the continental man of international business lost his composure and went all to pieces. In a flash, his fancy Bernini suit was lying in a pile on the floor. His hands trembled as he worked the catch of my bra. When he opened it and my tits fell out, he gasped audibly. Bending, he started sucking on one of my nipples.

Roughly, I took his head in my hands and pulled him away. "The panties," I commanded. "The *pantalóni.* Take them off, too." He obliged instantly, stripping the lacy undergarment from me. By now I was so excited that the crotch clung for a moment to the wet tissue of my open pussy. As he snatched the panties from my ankles, he lifted them to his face in a dramatic gesture and buried his nose in them, inhaling deeply.

"Ah," he murmured. "Perfume of the goddess."

"Eat it," I ordered, grabbing his shoulders and pushing down until he was on his knees. I tangled my fingers in his hair and pulled his face against my groin, moving my hips in circles to wash his lips with the dew that I knew was flowing from my opening. He took the cue and began to lick and suck.

I'm a lucky woman, because I get off real fast and easy, like a man. After he had been eating my pussy for less than a minute, I felt a climax starting and I just let it go. I flow quite a lot when I come, so I knew that I was covering his lips and mouth with the juices of my orgasm.

As soon as I was finished, I yanked him up by the hair and pushed him back onto the bed. His cock was thick and hard and standing straight up like a cannon from his jungle of shiny black pubic hair. I bent over it and took it in my mouth for a minute, licking and sucking it to get it well lubed. I wanted the taste of it to be clinging to my lips the way the taste of my pussy was clinging to his.

Then I climbed over him onto the bed and straddled him, poised with my opening just above his swaying hard-on. Gradually, I settled down into place, letting it find its way inside me. At the same time, I pressed my lips to his and kissed him deeply. I could taste my own flavors on his mouth and hoped he could taste his on mine. I always find it intoxicating to smell and taste my own juices while I fuck a man.

I led the movements, humping and pumping with my hips. I buried the length of his swollen rod in the depths of my guts and then moved slowly up again so that he practically came out of me. A sound, almost like a sob, came from his throat, as though he feared that his good fortune would slip away as my pussy pulled free of his cock. Before that could happen, though, I reversed direction and drove him deep again.

I was already beginning to feel another orgasm building. That made me speed up my movements so that I was bouncing against him like a locomotive. He reached up and grabbed my nipples, trying to steady me, to slow me down. All it did was make me hotter and drive me to move more quickly. I knew that he wanted to hold out, to keep himself in check and make it last, but I wasn't having it. I wanted what I wanted, and I wanted it right then!

"I'm coming," I moaned in his ear. "With you or without you," With that, I just let it go.

The spasms of my pussy and the sounds of my satisfaction must have done the trick for him, because I felt his cock beginning to spurt within seconds. *"Sì, sì, sì . . ."* he whispered hoarsely. *"Bène! Bène! Bène!"*

The only thing that comes close to the feeling I get when I'm coming is the feeling I get when a man is coming in me. Now I was getting both at the same time. It felt wonderful. More than that. It was what I needed. It's what I always need.

We kept fucking, even after the orgasms were over, driving our bodies together and apart until his cock went soft and slipped out of me with a muffled plop. Then I rolled over and lay next to him, breathing hard and coasting down from the heights I had reached. A few minutes later, I got up and started dressing.

I could feel his cum dripping out of me to wet the crotch of my panties when I put them on. I knew I would carry that moisture around with me for the rest of the day. It was a feeling I loved. With any luck at all, there would be another man to fill me before I had a chance to drain.

"Come on," I said. "You don't want to miss your plane."

Reluctantly, he got up and began putting his clothes on. "I'll never forget this trip," he said, trying to regain some of the continental charm that had somehow been squelched by the suddenness of our fuck. When he had adjusted his tie and slipped into his expensive Italian loafers, he reached into his pocket and took out a wad of American bills. "I won't have a chance to change these to lire," he said, holding the bundle out to me. "So I want you to have it."

I stared coldly at his outstretched hand for a moment before accepting the offering. "I'll consider it a tip for the haircut," I said. "Now run along and catch your plane."

"I'd like to write to you," he said, gazing into my face with his dark, velvet eyes.

"Don't," I answered. "Accept what happened for what it was.

We're just ships that passed in the night." I unlocked the front door and he was gone.

I haven't had another customer since he left, but the day isn't over yet. As soon as this interview is done, I'm hoping another man will come in to kill a little time. Telling you all this made me horny again.

6

ADVENTURE

EVERYONE LOVES AN ADVENTURE. DEFINED AS A NO-
vel or exciting event, adventure is what raises life above the humdrum or ordinary. It gives each of us something to anticipate with
pleasure, something to which we can joyfully look forward. Adventure carries with it a sense of danger, the rapid heartbeat and
shallow respiration that are inspired by confrontation with the unknown.

Some adventures are planned, guided, regimented, and con-
fined to tracks, like the cars of a roller coaster. Others come as an
electrifying surprise, like the excited panic that accompanies a sudden brake failure when driving down a curving mountain road.
Both kinds may leave us damp with perspiration and a new glad-
ness at being alive.

Like the other adventurous experiences of life, erotic adventures may erupt in all varieties. Some happen unexpectedly, like
the incident described by Valerie in this chapter. Others are actively sought, like the one encountered by Dick, who also tells his
story here. Either way, an adventure may imbue the person who
experiences it with a new sense of excitement. For some, secrecy
adds to this excitement.

CORPORATE WIFE

Valerie, twenty-one, is five feet nine inches tall with a figure that is meaty but manages to maintain classic proportions. Her breasts are full; her hips are wide; her bottom is firm and softly rounded. She wears her long blond hair in a single thick braid that reaches nearly to her waist. Her pale blue eyes gaze intently at the person to whom she is speaking, drawing the listener deep into her world. She works part-time as a bagger in a supermarket in a quiet neighborhood of a large metropolitan area.

Arthur and I have been married for about six months now. Before that, we lived together for almost a year. We've known each other since high school. I was his first girlfriend. He wasn't my first boyfriend, though. He's the same age as I am, but he was a virgin when we first got together. He doesn't know it, but I wasn't. I've had lots more sexual experience than he. Sometimes I feel as though I have to train him to be a good partner. He has so much to learn.

Still, there are times when our sex is fantastic. He's so full of exuberance and enthusiasm that it makes up for his lack of knowledge. He throws himself into it completely. In fact, he gets so excited that our lovemaking can be pretty intense. He likes me to dominate him, and I like doing it.

Sometimes, I see him watching me as I get dressed or undressed. I'll stand naked in front of the mirror combing my hair, very much aware that he is staring at me. He'll be sitting there on the edge of the bed, also naked, his eyes riveted to my body. After a while, I'll turn and ask, "Well, do you like what you see?"

"Oh, yes," he'll answer with that big shit-eating grin on his face.

Then I'll sit on my vanity bench and deliberately spread my thighs so he gets a good look between my legs. I can see him practically drooling with desire, but I have him trained to wait for my command. I'll stroke myself idly, running the tips of my fingers through my thick bush of pubic hair and maybe spreading my woman lips apart a little to let him peek inside me. "Want it?" I'll ask teasingly.

"Oh, yes," he'll say again, a look of earnest desire coming over his face.

"All right, then," I'll invite. "Get down on your knees and come over here for a closer look." I love to watch him cross the room on his knees to take up a position between my thighs. Then I like to look down and watch the expression on his face as he stares right into my opening.

"Sniff it," I'll say. "But be careful. No contact. Not yet." He'll lean forward and place his face just a fraction of an inch from me. Sometimes I can see the tips of my curling pubic hairs tickling his nose and feel his hot breath against my flowering lips. He'll inhale deeply, savoring the spicy scent of my sex. I'll see his cock twitching and dancing as the erotic fragrance fills his head.

"All right," I'll say after watching the look of torment on his face for a few moments. "You can taste it. But lightly. Very lightly." He knows what I expect and he gives it to me. Barely moving his head, he thrusts his tongue way out so the tip of it just grazes over the swollen lips of my pussy. I watch as he swabs up and down the length of my slit, each upstroke bringing him closer and closer to my clit.

By now I'm so excited that it's all purple and puffing out of the little tent that covers it. He looks at it lovingly and then begins to lick. Sometimes, I'll make him lick me that way until I come, without allowing him to use his hands or any other part of his body. I shudder when he gives me an orgasm, but I stay pretty quiet. I don't know whether he's ever sure I've had one. I like to keep him guessing. It makes him even more submissive.

After he's licked me to my satisfaction, I reach down and take his cock in my hand. "Would you like to put this inside me?" I tease. "Would you like to fuck me?"

"Oh, yes," he says again, in that dumb, sheeplike way that he has.

"How would you like to fuck me?" I ask, teasing him a little more before giving him what he wants. "Me on top? You on top? Standing up? Sitting down? Want to put it in my mouth? How do you want it?"

By now he's so aroused that he'd be thrilled to fuck me any way I'd let him—in the middle of a forest fire if necessary. Besides, he knows that it's completely up to me, not him. I like to be comfortable, so I usually lead him to the bed. I make him stand there at the foot of it while I lie down on my back and carefully arrange my legs so that they are splayed wide apart, giving him a clear view of my dripping puss.

I stretch my arms out and beckon with my crooked fingers. "Come on," I say softly. "What are you waiting for? Come and give me a good fucking." That's something he never fails to do. He's strong and healthy and he fucks me with such power that he always makes me come again.

I just love it when he comes, because although I have quiet climaxes with him, he raises holy hell. He hollers and shouts in ecstasy, repeating over and over, "I'm coming, I'm coming, I'm coming." It makes me feel wonderful to bring him such satisfaction and to have him bend completely to my will.

But a girl doesn't want to be in charge all the time. There are times I really wish he'd show a little more spunk and take control. Maybe that's why I got involved with Mr. X.

Arthur has an entry-level job with a pretty big company. He's just a sales trainee at the moment, but the word is that he'll have a brilliant future. They say a man can't succeed in the corporate world unless he has the right kind of wife. I've resolved to do my best to make sure that Arthur gets what we both deserve.

A few months ago, he was invited to a company party, and of course I went with him. It was in a very fancy ballroom in a classy part of town. Everybody there positively glittered. At one point, Arthur introduced me to some of the company executives. One, the one I'm referring to as Mr. X, seemed to take a special interest in me.

I was wearing a tight dress that really showed off my figure. It was rather low-cut, and I noticed Mr. X taking every possible opportunity to look down the neckline at my breasts. His glance felt like hot fingers, causing me to feel all flushed and warm. When he asked Arthur if he could dance with me, I felt flattered by his attention. Gracefully, we glided out onto the dance floor.

I'd say Mr. X is in his late forties. He's quite handsome and distinguished-looking. That night, he was wearing formal clothes. The fit was perfect, as though the suit was made for him. It probably was. He has thick, dark hair that he wears swept back from his forehead. He gives the appearance of power. It was obvious to me from his grooming and from the way he carried himself that he held an important position in the company.

As we danced, he told me that his wife hates social gatherings and never comes to company parties. He held me close to him as we whirled to the music, welding my breasts to his powerful chest. I thought I could feel the trace of an erection pressing against my thigh. His breath was warm on my cheek.

When the music ended, he whispered in my ear, "Valerie, you are a very exciting woman. Will you dance with me again later?" I just nodded as he led me back to where Arthur was waiting and handed me back to my husband.

As Mr. X walked away in the direction of the bar, Arthur told me that he was the company's director of personnel and that to a great extent he controlled Arthur's career. I mentioned as casually as I could that Mr. X said he wanted to dance with me again, and Arthur responded by saying, "Yes, by all means dance with him. It can only help." I was aware that Mr. X had something more than dancing in mind, but I don't think the idea ever entered my husband's innocent head.

About half an hour later, Mr. X found us again. Now, instead of asking Arthur's permission, as he had the first time, he asked me directly if I would dance with him. I smiled and glanced at my husband, who smiled back and said, "Have a ball."

While dancing, Mr. X held me even closer than he had before.

The warmth of his body was contagious. I soon found myself breathing heavily and glowing with excitement. "You look beautiful in that dress," he murmured. "I'll bet you look even better without it."

His boldness was a refreshing contrast to Arthur's timidity. It made me feel weak and vulnerable. I blushed and stammered. "What are you wearing under it?" he continued. "If I find a place where we can be alone, will you show me?"

I had no idea how to respond to his question, but he didn't wait for an answer. Taking me by the hand, he led me briskly toward the bar and then around it to a small room off the main ballroom. As we stepped inside, he flipped a handle, locking the door. "We only have a minute," he said. "So all I'll be able to do is look. Now lift your skirt and let me see your panties."

I had no thought of resistance. I remember that the only thing that passed through my mind was that I was glad I had worn a lacy set of pink undies. I knew they were sexy. Slowly, I complied with his command, taking the hem of my skirt in my hands and lifting it gradually. The idea of being dominated this way by a strong, powerful man excited me tremendously.

I hate panty hose and always go bare-legged no matter how formally I'm dressed. I raised the skirt until it was around my waist, knowing that he could see my pale bush through the pink lace. He just stood there with an approving look on his face.

"Now show me your bra," he ordered. The curtness of his command made my pussy wet and my nipples hard. No man had ever spoken to me in such a dominating way. I loved it. Dropping the skirt, I reached for the straps of my dress and slipped them down over my shoulders, lowering the top until it was around my waist. My big breasts filled the cups of the lacy pink bra, and I was fully aware of the twin shadows made by my dark erect nipples.

"Nice," he said. "Very nice. Next time, I'm going to want to see the rest of you." Licking his lips, he reached down and stroked the front of his trousers, showing me the bulge made by his erection. "Now get dressed," he said. "We've been in here long enough."

When I found Arthur, I was so flushed I was sure he would notice, but he never said a word. We stayed at the party for another hour and then left for home. By the time we got there, I was so hot from thinking about my little adventure with Mr. X that I practically raped my husband. In bed, I climbed over him and thrust him in me without any preliminary, fucking like mad until both of us were spent.

The next morning, Arthur told me that he was being sent to a training seminar that day. He said that Mr. X, who had chosen him specially for the assignment, told him about it the previous night just as we were leaving the party. He warned me that he wouldn't be home until late at night. When he left, I wondered how long it would be before I heard from Mr. X. I didn't wonder for long.

At about ten A.M., the phone rang. I answered it with a pounding heart, somehow knowing that it was him. With no introduction or formality, he said, "Meet me at the Marriott at noon. And don't be late." Then he mentioned a room number and hung up without another word.

I was shaking as I bathed and dressed for the rendezvous. I put on a teeny, sexy black bra and brief matching panties that Arthur bought for me the previous Christmas. I had never gotten around to wearing the set for him and now I'd be wearing it for his boss. Over the seductive underwear, I dressed in a sleek pantsuit made of shiny black material. I quickly braided my hair and was off.

I could hear my heart beating as I drove through the city and looked for a place to park. I was at least half an hour early and wasn't sure whether I should go to the room or spend some time in the cocktail lounge. I was afraid to be in public, though, afraid that my nervousness would show and that everybody would stare at me, so I decided to take a chance. In the elevator, I started to have second thoughts. I wasn't sure I could really go through with it. Then I thought of the authority in Mr. X's voice on the phone when he commanded me to meet him and I knew I had no choice.

I knocked timidly on the door and heard movement inside. Without preamble, it opened wide. There stood Mr. X in a white satin robe. "Come in," he said. "You look beautiful." I was shaking so hard I thought I'd fall down. As if he could read my mind, he went to a sideboard and turned to hand me a glass of wine, already poured and waiting for me. I just stood there, dumbfounded, sipping it and flustered as could be.

When I had finished the wine, he said, "Unbraid your beautiful hair. I want to see it soft and flowing, loose and free." His words sent a little shiver through me. There was something poetically masculine about the way he spoke. I did as he bid me, shaking my long blond hair and running my fingers through it as it fell from confinement.

"Now take off the pantsuit. I love the way you look in your underthings and I want to see you that way again."

I obeyed wordlessly, my trembling fingers fumbling at the buttons and zippers that held my clothing in place. In moments, I was clad in nothing but the black undies. He just stood there staring. Then, his eyes locked to mine, he untied the sash that held his robe and let it fall open. His cock, long and stiff, sprang out of the opening. Involuntarily, I found myself gazing at it.

"Come here and suck this," he said. His voice was quiet but firm. A thrill passed over me. Sensing my vulnerability, he snapped his fingers and gestured impatiently toward his prick. All I knew was that I wanted it in my mouth. I wanted to be his sex slave.

Advancing toward him, I bent at the waist and took his huge cock in my mouth. I started sucking, hard at first, and then soft, and then hard again. "Good," he murmured. "Yes, like that. Yes, that's just the way I like it."

I wanted to show him how good I could be. I fluttered my

tongue over the head of his hard-on, tasting the spicy flavor of his sex. His hands held my ears, gently but firmly, working my head forward and back as I mouthed his cock. I could feel it swelling as his balls churned forth a load.

When I give Arthur blowjobs, he's always careful to pull it out of my mouth before coming. But Mr. X wanted something more. Grasping the back of my head, he forced me to continue sucking him as he began to spurt. I could feel the hot liquid coursing from his cock into my mouth, filling it and working its way down my throat. I had never swallowed a man's cum before. Doing so made me feel totally submissive and completely like a woman. Awkwardly, I liked it.

He kept working my head forward and back until his climax was complete. Then, cupping my chin in one powerful hand, he raised me to a standing position and kissed me deeply on the mouth, his tongue plunging into the spot where his prick had been just a moment before. His hands worked expertly to remove my bra and free my breasts, which he began stroking and petting with a sort of controlled roughness.

I was amazed to feel his cock getting hard again, pressing against the soft skin of my belly. Without breaking lip contact, he started shuffling forward, working me back until I was standing next to a desk in a corner of the room. Turning me around with his hands, he bent me over it, so that my naked breasts were pressed against the smooth, shiny surface. My panty-covered ass was sticking out behind me, inviting anything he might choose to do.

I felt his hands pull my panties to one side, exposing my hot wet pussy. Then, with a long smooth stroke, he drove his erect cock into me, not stopping until it was buried as far as it could go. I gasped in pleasure.

He started to move his hips forward and back in a sawing motion, driving himself relentlessly in and out of my pussy. His hands held my waist and pulled me back against him as he plunged hard and fast. I heard myself shouting as the head of his cock bumped my cervix. I had never felt so full before, never been so fulfilled. I was making loud, boisterous, unintelligible sounds as he fucked me from behind. "God, yes," I wailed. "Oh, God, yes. Fuck me. Fuck me."

When my orgasm struck, I positively screamed. Shrieked. Moaned. Groaned. Oh, it was the mightiest orgasm ever. It was the only climax the world had ever known. Oh, if only it could go on forever. Oh, I won't be able to stand another second. Oh, give me more. Oh, stop, I can't stand it. Oh, no. Oh, more. Oh, no more.

Mr. X humped against me without regard to the sounds I was making, driving deeper and deeper until he was ready to come again. It seemed to go on forever. Then he let it fly. I could feel the hot whirling jets of semen shooting from the tip of his cock to splash against the walls of my womb. It felt like I was being fucked by a giant.

Later we lay together in the bed and fucked some more. And then we fucked still more. Mr. X was always in control, and I was always willing to do as he commanded. By the time night came, I was totally worn out and more satisfied than I ever thought possible.

As I was dressing to leave, he said, "I think your husband is going to be sent out of town on a somewhat regular basis. I'm going to want you to meet me here fairly often. Just make sure you come when I call." Then almost as an afterthought, he said, "I think your husband has a great future with our company."

When Arthur got home that night, I was in bed sleeping, totally exhausted. When I heard him come in, though, I rolled over, spreading my legs. "Fuck me, Arthur," I said in a drowsy voice. The contrast would be exciting.

I've been enjoying that contrast ever since. At home, I'm dominant, and my partner is my slave. He'll do anything I want him to do, and nothing makes him happier than serving me. With Mr. X, I'm the submissive one. I take his orders and commands and find myself doing things with him that I'd never think of on my own. That's what makes my affair with him such an exciting adventure.

HOT TUB

Dick stands six feet four inches and has a muscular physique, with broad shoulders and a powerful chest. He says it comes from weight training at the gym three or four times a week whenever he's in town. He is thirty-eight, with sandy brown hair and big hazel eyes. His teeth are pearly white and perfectly straight. He insists that no work has ever been done on them. His olive skin draws tight across high cheekbones. When he smiles, little crinkles appear at the corners of his eyes. A small diamond stud flashes in the lobe of one ear.

Becky and I have been married for eight years. She's four years younger than I am. I was married once before, but it was a disaster that lasted less than a year. I guess we were both very young and too immature for marriage. That's why I waited until I was thirty to remarry.

Becky and I have a sound relationship, with lots of good sex. She accepts our lifestyle, even though my job as a salesman takes me away from home a great deal. Thank goodness Becky isn't one of those women who complains that I'm hardly ever home. Instead she appreciates it when I am there.

When I travel, I always make it a point of bringing a little gift home for her. Nothing big, of course, but something that shows her that I'm thinking of her. Maybe that keeps me from feeling guilty about the sexual adventures I have when I'm out of town.

I'm a good salesman. My boss says I could sell ice to Eskimos, and he's right. He sends me all over the country for the difficult sales. I learned a long time ago that seduction is just a matter of salesmanship. I'm every bit as good with the ladies as I am with sales prospects. No matter where I go, I can pretty much count on finding a woman to spend a few sexy hours with. I think it's the reason I love my job as much as I do.

I'm very careful to keep my adventures from finding their way home. I guard my identity and I never fool around with women I do business with. Always strangers. For one thing, that makes it more challenging. For another, it's safer.

Usually I go to a singles bar, the kind of place that's known as a meat market. It's funny, because everybody thinks that these are the places where sexual connections are made, but that really isn't true. Most of the people who frequent those places are hoping to get lucky, but very few of them ever do. The men tend to be about as subtle as sledgehammers, and that turns the women off. So even though the atmosphere always reeks of sex, most of the people who go there with big plans end up disappointed and end up sleeping alone.

I've got a way about me, though. I know I can always find something. That makes my attitude a little less urgent than that of the other guys. I think it shows in some subtle way that even I don't understand. Usually, all I have to do is sit at the bar and order a drink, without paying too much attention to what's going on around me. I'm not the least bit desperate. That's probably why it doesn't take long before some woman will come along and sit down beside me to start a conversation.

I'm always polite, but my attitude is that I can take it or leave it. I think that's what intrigues them. Nine times out of ten, I score. What I mean is I end up leaving with a woman I've only known for a few minutes, destined for a night of hot sex. I've been doing it for ten years. I almost never miss.

I don't use my real name and I never take them back to my own hotel. I like to keep it as anonymous as possible. So I just identify myself as Jim. I say I'm from out of town, without getting real specific. If they press, I might say I'm from the East Coast and let it go at that. Or if I happen to be on the East Coast, I might say I'm from the West Coast. I guess I've been doing it so long that it just comes natural to me.

Some of the women I meet that way are pretty mediocre, but I don't really care. It's the adventure that counts. Once in a while, I hit upon a really special one that I remember for years afterwards. I'm thinking about one of those right now.

It was a couple of years ago, I guess. I was in Hawaii, attending a sales conference at a fancy hotel on the Big Island. One evening, I rented a car and drove into the town of Kona, where the bars and cocktail lounges line up shoulder to shoulder against the ocean. I picked a likely looking joint and went in. Sitting at the bar, I ordered one of those exotic drinks that Hawaii is famous for. A mai tai, or a sex-on-the-beach, or a blue passion; one of those.

The place was crowded and noisy, but I managed to block it all out. I just sat quietly at the bar, sipping. Before long, a willowy blonde came up and perched on the bar stool next to mine. She was holding a glass in her hand, but it was almost empty. "Hi," she said. "I'm Cindy. You look lonely."

"Well, Cindy," I answered with a bit of a sigh. "I'm a long way from home." Then, glancing at her glass, I asked, "Can I get you a refill?" Without waiting for an answer, I signaled to the bartender. He seemed to know her, because he refilled her drink without asking what she was having.

She and I chatted for a few minutes, mainly about the ocean and the weather and the view. Just idle bullshit with no particular end in sight. We both finished our drinks at the same time. I was getting ready to order another round, when she said, "You aren't married to this bar, are you? Want to get out of here?"

"Sure," I said. "You have a place around here?"

"I'm renting a condo," she answered. "We can go back there. You like hot tubs? There's a nice one."

"Sounds good to me," I said. "Although I don't have a bathing suit or anything."

She grinned. "Oh, I think we'll make out," she said, a sly tone creeping into her voice.

She told me a friend had dropped her off and she didn't have a car with her, so we drove to her place in my rental. We went straight to her apartment. She wasted no time. As soon as we got inside, she wrapped her arms around me and pressed her lips to mine. It was a long, torrid kiss, with plenty of tongue and lots of nibbling. I found myself becoming aroused almost at once.

She giggled, pressing her crotch against my hard-on. "Anxious, aren't we?" she said teasingly. "Let's see what you've got." With that, she unzipped my pants and reached in for my cock. I was all tangled up in my underwear, and it took her a few seconds to find her way through the jumble. When she did, her touch was so light and soft that I felt myself growing bigger and thicker.

Stepping back, she began pulling at her own clothing, practically ripping it off. She was naked before I knew what was happening. I followed suit and peeled out of my clothes, too. I reached for her, my hand going for her pussy. I was a little surprised to discover that she was totally shaved down there. There was something especially exciting about the way her sex was right out there for me to see and touch, with no barrier of any kind to block the path.

She let me stroke it for a moment, becoming wet as my fingers found their way inside her hairless slit. My other hand went for her breasts. They were small and cone-shaped, the nipples coming to hard points of pale pink. As I fingered her pussy and stroked her tits, she sighed. I felt her hand wrapping around my cock and thought we were going to do it right there on the floor.

But then she stepped back. "No," she said. "Not here. Let's get into the hot tub." I was a little taken aback, because I was all primed and ready to fuck. I didn't see how it would be possible in a communal swimming area. "Every apartment in this section has its own," she explained. "Come on, it's right outside on the patio."

The idea was exciting. Our own private little spa for soaking and sex. I let her lead me through the sliding glass doors that opened to her patio. I was surprised again, though, because nothing but a low picket fence separated her patio from the one belonging to the neighboring apartment. As we walked nude to the hot tub, I could see and hear that there were people in the tub next door. The moon was bright and almost full, so I knew that our naked bodies were totally visible to them, just as their bodies were visible to us.

They were a young couple, looking to be in their early twenties. They watched us openly, making no pretense about their interest. Both were rather attractive. Their stares were making me feel a little uncomfortable. I climbed into the tub as fast as I could to hide myself in the bubbling water. Cindy took her sweet time, though. She seemed to enjoy showing herself off to them. As she stepped over the rim of the redwood tub, she positioned herself deliberately with open legs facing them, so they could look right into her crotch.

As she did this, the young woman in the other tub stood up and leaned way over to get a better look. She was naked, too, with huge boobs that hung down as she bent forward. Keeping her eyes on Cindy, she reached back and grabbed her partner's hand, pulling him to his feet so he could get a better look. His cock was stiff and swaying from side to side. I felt a little flustered.

"Tell you what," Cindy said, addressing all of us at the same time. "We'll watch you and you can watch us. Okay?" Without waiting for an answer, she sank into the heated water, settling herself on my lap with her chest against my chest. The tip of my cock was trapped between her thighs, which she pressed tightly together around it.

Reaching around her, I took her pointy tits in my hands and began stroking and petting them. There was something unusually exciting about knowing that the couple in the other tub were watching me do it. As I felt Cindy's nipples harden to diamond points of desire, I could see the young man playing with his lady's big tits, pressing them together and cupping them in his hands, forcing her swollen nipples to jut out from between his fingers.

Cindy's hand was between her thighs now, holding my cock and rubbing it lightly up and down. Moving her hips just slightly, she managed to lift herself and, with her hand, to insert me into her waiting pussy. The inside felt even hotter and wetter than the bubbling water of the tub.

As soon as my cock was all the way in her, she uttered a scream of delight, obviously designed to attract the attention of the other couple. I could see them looking at us intently. Cindy began rocking her body forward and back, letting me guide her with my hands on her tits. Each movement brought me deeper inside her. Each time she settled down against my lap, she issued another little cry of pleasure.

The sounds she was making coupled with the situation and the sensations emanating from my swollen cock were beginning to overpower me. I was losing myself in the pure lust of the moment. Vaguely, I was aware that the woman in the other tub had stood up and was bending over with her hands on the rim while her partner entered her from behind. Through half-closed eyes, I saw them fucking with long powerful strokes. At the same time, Cindy's movements were bringing me to orgasm.

I started to grunt as the torrents of cum began pouring from my nuts. I fired shot after shot into her waiting body, while she groaned and sobbed to let me know she was coming too. We kept it up for a long time before I settled back to let the heated water soak through me as the tension left. I let my eyes close and lay there absorbing the good feelings for a long period of time. When I opened my eyes, the young couple next door were still fucking.

When the other couple finished their screwing, Cindy climbed out of the tub, careful to show them her ass as she did so. Taking my hand she pulled me after her. "Let's go back inside," she said. "I want a drink."

Inside the apartment, she made us a couple of cocktails, and we drank them, still naked. As soon as our glasses were drained, she said, "Well, what do you think? Are you ready for more sex?" Frankly, I didn't think I would be, but I was wrong. She looked at me hungrily and licked her lips, letting one hand stray over the still wet mound of her shaved pussy. I was hard in an instant.

"This time, in bed," she said, leading the way into the bedroom. We fucked two or three more times that night. Whenever I started to feel like I just didn't have the energy to continue, I'd think about the earlier scene outside, when we were watching the other couple fucking while they were watching us. It would get me hard all over again.

I've been with lots of women, but this was one of the best sessions I can ever remember. It's because when I'm getting laid, we usually don't have company, and we usually don't have an audience. There was something so erotic about the casual way Cindy had invited the strangers to watch us that it has stayed with me ever since.

I left just before the sun came up. Of course I've never seen or heard from Cindy again. That's the way I like it. I keep the adventures a million miles away from home. Except in my head. Sometimes, when Becky and I are making love and I close my eyes, I'm picturing one of the women I've met on my sales trip. More often than not, it's Cindy.

7

MY PARTNER
WON'T DO
WHAT I WANT

SOME STATES PROHIBIT SEXUAL ACTS IDENTIFIED ONLY
as "the crime against nature," or "the detestable and abominable
crime against nature." In 1975, a Tennessee man who had been
convicted of violating this prohibition after performing oral sex on
his neighbor, went to the United States Supreme Court, arguing
that the law was not specific enough to inform a reasonable person
of what conduct was illegal. The high court disagreed, referring
to an old English statue that used the same expression and was
historically understood to prohibit anal sex, oral sex, mutual masturbation, and various other erotic practices then regarded as unusual.

Today such laws still exist, although the acts involved are generally recognized to be common. We are tempted to ask this question: If creatures of nature do something, how can it be against
nature? By analogy: Is the Aswan Dam any less natural than a
beaver dam, simply because it was built by animals with two legs
rather than four? Although the laws that prohibit noncommercial
sex practices between consenting adults are rarely enforced, many
people continue to regard the acts involved as unholy, dirty, or
unnatural.

Perhaps this view is a perfectly valid one. Were we to criticize
it, we would be untrue to our resolution to remain nonjudgmental.

There is no doubt, however, that such a belief can lead to problems when one domestic partner holds it and the other does not. For some, the sex acts involved can be more satisfying than any others. If their mates disagree, they must either learn to accept a life in which they are denied the fulfillment they seek, or they must look for it outside their relationships.

Hayley and Gerald, whose stories are told in this chapter, took the latter route. Both are content with their spouses in all respects but one. Neither spouse is willing to engage in the acts that the partner finds most exciting. Hayley found herself turning to an old boyfriend for the satisfaction she craved, while Gerald renewed a relationship with a formerly casual acquaintance. What they have in common is that both feel the need to keep their hungers and their methods of nourishing them a secret.

SMALL TOWN

Although she is twenty-five, Hayley wears a look of youthful innocence. She says that she acquired it as part of her religious education. Hayley lives in a small town in America's Southeast and appears to fit right in with the fundamentalist lifestyle of her Bible Belt home. Her face is clean and well-scrubbed, without a trace of makeup. Her flaxen hair is brushed to a gleaming luster, worn long and loose, almost to her waist. Her gray-blue eyes peer out at the world as though seeing everything for the first time. She is slight of build, her trim figure hidden behind a crisp white blouse and shirtwaist.

I had a very strict religious upbringing, like most of the other girls around here. My family belongs to the local church. It's always been the center of our lives. We grew up knowing what God expected of us and exactly how to behave to make Him happy. My problem was, it just didn't work for me.

I was a little on the wild side. I couldn't help being rebellious. If a church meeting was supposed to start at nine sharp, I just had to get there at nine-thirty. If we were supposed to be silent, I always had something important to say to the person sitting next to me. If the occasion was solemn, I found something funny enough to make me laugh out loud.

When I was a young teenager, my parents were always scolding and punishing me to try to keep me in line. The harder they tried, the wilder I got. Finally I committed the ultimate act of rebellion. I started dating without their permission. To make it worse, the boy was somebody from outside our church.

I was eighteen already. In most cultures that would make me an adult, free to do what I wanted. But where I come from, a girl is subject to her parents' rule until she gets married. Even then, she doesn't get married without their approval. That didn't stop me, though.

I met Lewis when I took my daddy's car to get it filled with gas one Saturday morning. There isn't any filling station in our town, so it was necessary to drive twelve miles down the road. For me, it was a weekly outing, a chance to get away from the usual surroundings, even if only for an hour or so.

Lewis had just come to the area and was working at the gas station. I remember that first time we met. He was pumping gas into the tank. I was just sort of standing there next to him, when suddenly he said, "You're awful pretty. How about taking a walk with me a little later on, when I get off work?"

There was something strong and honest about him that attracted me immediately. It was the first time I had acknowledged any feeling other than friendship or contempt for a member of the opposite sex. I didn't quite understand it, but I liked the way it felt.

I explained that the car was my daddy's and it would be hard for me to get there without it. He said he would come to my town on his motorcycle and pick me up at home. "Oh, no," I said. "Not at home. I don't think Daddy would approve." So we made arrangements to meet near the church. I knew I could always find an excuse for going there in the evening.

That first time we got together, we just walked around in the fields outside of town. There was a bright moon. Lewis spent a bit of time talking about it, describing the way the moonlight made my face shine, and saying silly little romantic things like that. By the time he walked me back to the church and I headed home, I was already infatuated with him.

After that we found lots of opportunities to meet in the evenings. I think my mama suspected that I was seeing someone, but she never asked about it until later on. Lewis and I would walk in the countryside mostly, because I didn't want anyone to see us together. He wasn't of our church, and dating an outsider was a complete no-no in our community.

One night we were standing under a huge willow tree, with branches that pretty much isolated us from the rest of the world. Lewis took me in his arms and started to kiss me. I knew I should resist, but I just could not. The kiss went straight to my head, intoxicating me like a long drink of sabbath wine. Before I knew it, I was kissing him back. It's probably hard for you to believe that a girl of eighteen was experiencing her first kiss, but that's how it is in my home town.

The next time we met, we headed straight for that willow tree and started kissing almost at once. This time, his hands began moving over my body. I did nothing to stop him. When he cupped my breasts through my clothing, I felt a tingle that permeated my entire body. It seemed to center in my groin. I had never done anything like this before, but I had read books and magazines. I knew that we were doing what they call foreplay. It felt wonderful.

Lewis had brought a blanket with him and he spread it on the ground. Without a word, we both sank down onto it and began to embrace. My head was spinning with new sensations, feelings I had never experienced before. I let him unbutton my clothes and touch me all over. I even touched him, shocked by the hugeness of his organ as my hand groped for it through the open fly of his trousers.

Before I knew what was happening, we were both completely naked. His hand was between my legs, stroking and petting my most private place, burning me with the flames of excitement. I couldn't stop him. Or if I could, I didn't want to. I was totally consumed with the new experience, my body writhing involuntarily to the pleasure that he was bringing me.

Suddenly he whispered, "I want to make love to you now." He climbed on top of me. I felt his organ jabbing against me, looking for that wet spot between my legs.

My blood ran cold. It was bad enough that we were naked and petting, but now we were on the brink of actual sexual intercourse. I knew once that happened, I'd be soiled forever. As curious and hungry as I was for it, as much as I desired it, my upbringing stopped me from consummating that desire. Intercourse was something that had to be reserved for marriage. As an outsider, Lewis was someone I'd never be able to marry. As rebellious as I might have been, I just couldn't allow this to happen.

"No," I almost shouted, the panic rising in my voice. "No, I can't do this." I was afraid that he would be so carried away by his animal lusts that there would be no stopping him, that he'd force his way into me and sully me irrevocably. But he didn't. He was tender.

"It's all right," he crooned. "I won't do anything you don't want me to do. I just want you to feel good." As he whispered these words, he climbed off and lay beside me, his hands moving gently and slowly over my nakedness. Within moments, the fear left me. I knew I could trust him.

"Let me show you how wonderful your body can feel," he said softly. He was kissing me now. First he kissed my mouth. Then my breasts. His lips lingered over my swollen nipples, sucking gently on them. I felt eased, comforted by his attentions. Deep inside me there was a feeling of sorrow. I had been so close to sexual fulfillment. I damned the fear that had kept me from experiencing it.

Slowly, his lips trailed over my bare belly, making me tingle as he kissed and nibbled his way lower and lower. He was coming close to my private patch of hair. I couldn't imagine what he had in mind. He was just inches away from my secret opening. My heart was beating so hard I thought I would faint. Then he was kissing me *there!*

I couldn't believe it. *There!* My mind was racing. I had to stop him. This was wrong. So very, very wrong. That part of the body was not meant to be touched by the mouth. It couldn't be right. But the pleasure was incredible. Indescribable. How could this be happening? How could anything so wrong feel this good?

His lips were nibbling me now, each new touch bringing a wave of pleasure rolling over me. He seemed to be exploring me with his mouth, finding places I didn't even know existed. His tongue was teasing me, concentrating on one little button that seemed to grow bigger and bigger as he nuzzled and licked it. Involuntarily, I moved my legs to wrap my thighs around his head, afraid he might break the contact.

His tongue was plunging into me, driving in and out. He was performing intercourse on me with his mouth. Between thrusts, he was licking up and down and all around that little button. I was on fire, flames of panic and pleasure shooting up into my belly from the private center of my sex.

I was losing control. Something momentous was about to take place. Something I had never even known possible. I was turning completely inside out, my center exposed to God's heaven. I was terrified and mesmerized all at the same time. "Oh, God!" I screamed, not at all sure of what I was screaming about. "Oh, Lewis. Oh, yes!"

Suddenly something seemed to burst inside me. Something wonderful was happening. Something so big and powerful that there could be no stopping it. It was like a steamroller gone mad.

I was in a kind of convulsion, my body going all rigid and collapsing in a series of shuddering thuds that deafened me to all the sounds of the earth. I thought I might be dying and I just didn't care.

Afterwards I lay there, feeling like a completely changed person. I had been allowed to see the infinity of God's universe, if only for a moment. I would never forget the brilliance of the colors I saw and the music I heard as my soul went on its heavenly journey.

After that Lewis and I got together as often as possible. He never tried to have intercourse with me again. Instead he was content to press his mouth to my sex and bring me to that fabulous place again and again. Eventually, he taught me to do the same thing to him. The first time, it was awkward, taking his huge organ in my mouth and licking it until it spat. But I soon learned to love bringing him the same kind of ecstasy that he brought me.

It couldn't go on forever. One day, my mama took me aside and said she knew I had been seeing an outsider. "You're not a little girl anymore," she said. "Sooner or later, things will happen. Bad things. You mustn't see him anymore. You need to be thinking about marriage."

She and Daddy had picked out a boy for me to marry. You might not think so, but things are still done that way where I come from. I had known Garrett since childhood. We had been in the same church groups together for as long as I could remember. He was a nice boy, and I always enjoyed his company. He knew how to make me laugh and never looked at me with disapproval the way the other kids did when I cut up at Sunday school.

So I told Lewis I couldn't see him anymore and I started going out with Garrett. Since our parents had already worked things out, it didn't take long for our relationship to become serious. He proposed, and we were married on my twentieth birthday.

Before that, we never had any kind of sexual contact. In fact, our first kiss didn't happen until the preacher finished the ceremony by saying, "You may kiss the bride." It was kind of cold, without passion. I thought that was because of Garrett's lack of experience. Most folks who get married in our town don't have any sexual experience at all. They're supposed to learn together as husband and wife.

Garrett didn't learn much, though. During the first year of our marriage, sex was rare. It almost never happened unless I took the initiative, and then Garrett would let me know that he didn't exactly approve of my aggressiveness. But I had no choice. I needed more than he was interested in giving me.

When we did have sex, it was quick and uninspired. I'd try kissing him and stroking him for a while, but as soon as he got an erection, he'd want to stick it in me. Then he'd move a couple of times and it was all over. I tried getting him interested in oral sex, but the way he reacted, you would have thought I asked him to sleep with the devil.

Once, when he was half asleep, I slipped down and took his semihard penis in my mouth. He jumped up and out of bed as though I had touched him with an electric wire. "Don't ever do that," he scolded. "God will punish us both." That was when I realized that our life would forever lack excitement.

For a few years, I tried to tell myself that I could live without sexual satisfaction. But it just didn't work. I'm a normal, healthy woman, and the frustration was beginning to make me bitter. When Garrett came home from work at the end of the day, he'd find an angry wife waiting for him. If he asked what was bothering me, I couldn't tell him. It wasn't something he would ever be able to understand.

After reading an article in a women's magazine, I tried masturbating. It didn't leave me satisfied, though. Instead, I felt kind of dirty. I didn't know what I was going to do.

Then, one day, while I was on a shopping trip in the city, about sixty miles from home, I ran into my old boyfriend, Lewis. He was working behind the counter in a coffee shop where I stopped in for lunch. As soon as he spotted me, he slipped into the booth where I was sitting and said, "Oh, Hayley, I'm so glad to see you.

You have no idea how much time I spend thinking about you. Tell me about your life. Are you happy?"

I didn't feel I could tell Lewis or anyone the truth about my sexless marriage, so I just mouthed platitudes about family and the weather. Lewis was not as reticent as I. He described his situation to me quite frankly. He said he had gotten married a few years earlier and was absolutely miserable. He referred to his wife as a "frigid iceberg," saying that she had no interest in sex whatsoever. He admitted that when he was lying in bed at night frustrated and filled with desire, his mind would return to those evenings we used to spend having oral sex beneath the stars.

Somehow, and I'm still not sure of exactly what was said to bring it about, we agreed to meet after he got off work. I waited around for a couple of hours and then met him in front of the coffee shop as planned. He took me to a cheap motel. I probably should have felt degraded, but I was so excited by the thought of receiving some sexual satisfaction that I didn't even notice the surroundings.

The minute we got into the room, we stripped off our clothes and leaped into the bed. He buried his face in my groin immediately and brought me to one sweet orgasm after another. Then I took a turn doing him.

Since then, life has improved for both of us. Garrett is a good husband in every aspect of life except the bedroom. He makes a good living and treats me with tenderness and respect. That's almost enough to satisfy me. For the rest, I get together with Lewis as often as possible.

Lewis and I never have intercourse; nothing but oral sex. We manage to pack enough orgasms into our afternoon meetings to make up for the times when we lie next to our unresponsive spouses. I guess I can't complain. One way or another, I'm getting what I need.

Gerald, who owns a tile store, is thirty-nine and beginning to take on a middle-aged look. He is five-foot-eleven, but appears shorter because of his stoop-shouldered posture. His brown hair is starting to go gray; his cheeks are a bit jowly; and he has developed a paunch that forces him to hitch his belt below his belly. His green eyes retain a youthful sparkle, though, when he reminisces about an experience he once had with his wife.

I guess it was about ten years ago. I was working as a tile setter. My good buddy, Ned, worked with me. My wife, Cara, and Ned's girlfriend, Ashley, were pretty close, too. They had known each other since high school. At this particular time, me and Cara had been married for maybe four or five years. Ned and Ashley had only been living together a few months.

After work on Fridays, me and Ned used to meet up with some other guys for a poker game. On this particular night, I made out pretty good. Just about cleaned everybody out. So I was feeling fine when we went back to Ned's place, where our women were waiting for us. They were feeling no pain themselves, having been doing a number on a jug of wine. As soon as we walked in, they poured us some and challenged us to catch up with them.

We drank and kidded around for a while, sitting at the table in their kitchen. Then Cara asked how the poker game went. Ned said, "Your husband was the big winner. He's just too good for the rest of us."

Cara whooped with joy. "Hallelujah," she hollered. "We're in the money."

Ned's girl, Ashley, said, "Hey, since you're such a hot poker player, maybe you ought to teach us a few things." I could see she was pretty drunk.

Now, I ought to tell you that I had known Ashley ever since we were teenagers. I never went out with her or anything, but I always kind of knew she had a thing for me. I don't know why nothing ever happened between us. She's a really hot-looking woman. She's blond and a little on the chunky side, but in a really sexy way, with big tits and a nice round ass that sticks out like an invitation. Lots of times I was tempted to pat it or grab it, and I don't think she would have minded. But she and Cara were such good friends that I always stopped myself.

"Yeah," Cara chimed in. "Why don't you show us how the game is played." Her speech was slurred, and I knew that she was every bit as drunk as Ashley.

"All right," I said. "Shall we play for pennies or something?"

"No way," Ashley sputtered. "Let's make it really interesting. How about a game of strip poker."

"I think that's a great idea," my wife said.

I guess Ashley was only kidding at first, but now that Cara had validated it, she started to get serious. "Yeah," Ashley repeated. "Strip poker it will be." She got up and went rummaging around in a kitchen drawer until she found a deck of cards. "Come on," she said. "Let's take this into the living room."

They had a couch and a love seat put together in an L-shape, so we settled down and I dealt a hand of five-card draw on the coffee table. As I passed out the cards, Ashley poured more wine for all of us. I was beginning to feel a little buzzed.

When Ashley lost the first hand, she casually slipped out of her blouse without saying a word. I found it pretty exciting to see her sitting there in her white bra, with her big tits overflowing the cups. I really didn't think it would go any further than that. She stayed cool when she lost the second hand, though. Grinning, she just reached around behind her, unsnapped the clip on her bra, and took it off.

There she was, with her big melons completely exposed. I just stared for a good long minute before reshuffling the cards. Suddenly, remembering the situation, I glanced at my buddy to see how he was taking it. To my surprise, he seemed to be enjoying himself. "Hey, Gerald," he said in a low voice. "Don't my lady have a great set of hooters?" His words had some kind of effect on Ashley, because I could see her nipples beginning to get hard.

I wanted to see more, so I dealt the next couple of hands as quick as I could. Ned lost them both. In a minute, he was sitting there in his undershirt and boxers. I could see my wife looking at his crotch, where his cock was starting to peek out from the open front of the shorts. Somehow, I didn't mind in the least. Ashley got up and moved around the table, her big boobs bobbing as she refilled everyone's glasses.

Cara lost the next hand and, without hesitation, shrugged out of her sweater. I lost the one after that and took off my shirt. Than Cara lost again. I wondered whether she was going to take off her bra the way Ashley had, but she took off her pants instead. Now she was perched cross-legged beside me wearing only bra and panties. I wasn't sure, but it looked to me as though the crotch of her cotton panties was a little damp. I wondered if the situation was exciting her as much as it was exciting me.

I kept dealing, and the clothes kept coming off, until Ned and Ashley were totally naked, and Cara and I were down to our underpants. My hands shook as I dealt the next hand. This time Cara lost. For a moment, I thought she might chicken out. But she didn't. Instead, she stood up and dramatically hooked her thumbs into the waistband of her panties. All eyes were on her as she slowly slipped them down over her hips and thighs. Now, she too was naked.

I can't quite explain it, but I felt a certain kind of crazy thrill at the thought of my wife appearing totally nude in front of our friends. The idea seemed to turn her on too, because I could see shining moisture on her pussy. Her bush seemed all wet and matted. She turned slowly in place before sitting down again, spreading her knees wide apart to allow a good clear view of her snatch. My cock was so hard, it was starting to ache.

"Hey," Cara said to me. "You're the only one who isn't nude. How about taking off your drawers like the rest of us." Swiftly, I did. It felt really good for all four of us to be sitting there totally naked.

"Too bad it's over," Ned said. "This really has been fun."

"Hey, it doesn't have to be over," his wife answered. "Let's keep going. Only now, the loser has to play with himself while the rest of us watch. Himself or herself, that is."

"Great idea," I said, dealing out another hand. Ned was the loser. As soon as he tossed his cards in, he leaned back and began stroking his cock for all of us to see. I don't mind telling you, it was a very exciting moment. Not that the sight of Ned or his cock was turning me on. It was the whole situation. The idea of four people sitting around, totally naked, watching as he jerked himself off was really arousing. I felt like I wanted to stroke my own cock for everyone, too. And to see the women rubbing their pussies.

As if she had read my mind, Ashley said, "Let's not mess with these cards anymore. Why not just let's do it." With that, she leaned back and began petting the thick blond bush that surrounded her sex. I don't think I've ever seen such a full hairy wad on a woman. She ran her fingers through the curls and then slipped one fingertip between the lips of her pussy.

"Come on, Cara," she said. "We all know you want to."

Once again, all eyes were on my wife. She stopped to take a sip from her wineglass. Then she began to imitate Ashley, rubbing her own pubic hair and sliding her fingers up and down her slit. I didn't even have to think about it. My hand was wrapped around my cock and pumping up and down for all I was worth.

I don't think I ever was that riled up before in my life. Watching my wife masturbate in front of the others was in-fucking-credible. I rubbed my cock harder and harder. As I stroked myself, I looked around the room. It felt so free and exciting to be doing this in front of everyone else. I liked it when I saw them looking my way. And I liked looking at them.

Ashley's fingers were whirling expertly around her clit. I could see it standing up thick and red as she nudged and tickled it with a fingertip. Below it, her lips were all turned out and coated with a thick glistening moisture. She kept dipping into it to wet the little button as she rolled it around and around.

Cara had stiffened two fingers and was driving them in and out of her pussy, fucking herself with abandon. Her head was thrown back and her eyes were tightly shut. She was beyond performing. She was just giving herself a good time. I was fascinated by the sight of it. In all the years of our marriage, I had never seen her jerking off before.

Suddenly I was distracted by a low grunting sound coming from Ned. I glanced at him and saw his hand driving furiously up and down on his stiff cock. He was gasping for breath. Then, suddenly, he began to spurt. Huge gobs of hot gism shot from the tip of his swollen prick and flew through the air, splashing on his girlfriend's naked belly.

As she got a bath from his cum, Ashley began to let go. "Oh," she sobbed. "I'm coming, too." I could see by the expression on Cara's face that she was starting to orgasm at the same time. I didn't know where to look first.

Then my eyes closed as my climax started. Boom, bang. I was shooting cum all over the place, feeling it flow through my fingers and dribble down over my balls. I kept jerking until I was totally saturated. When it was over, I settled back onto the cushions of the couch and tried to catch my breath.

For a long moment, the room was filled with silence. Then someone started to laugh. Before I knew it we were all hysterical, giggling and guffawing and laughing out loud. It had been so much fun that we just couldn't contain it.

We sat around naked for quite a while sipping more wine and staring into space. Quietly, Ned started stroking his cock again. Pretty soon, we were all doing it. It was every bit as great as it had been the first time.

When it was done, I felt so sleepy, I wasn't sure I'd be able to make it home. Fortunately, we only lived a couple of doors away from Ned and Ashley. Tossing our clothes on carelessly, we hurried home and ran into the bedroom. Cara and I were both too wiped out for sex, so we just fell asleep in each other's arms.

The next morning, Cara was wearing a serious expression. "I want to talk about last night," she said, as we sat down for coffee. I could tell from her tone that there was trouble coming. "I had a real good time," she said. "But I was drunk. A lot drunker than I should have let myself get. I don't know how I'm going to face Ashley and Ned. I don't even know how I can face myself in the mirror."

I tried to soothe her, telling her that Ashley and Ned were our good friends and that there was nothing to be embarrassed about. I was hoping we'd be able to do the same thing again, and I told her so. But Cara was adamant. "No way," she said. "No way in hell will that ever happen again."

That was that! For weeks afterwards, I tried to get my wife to change her mind, but she absolutely wouldn't budge. I tell you, it broke my heart, because I had more fun that night than I ever had before. I just couldn't see how I could live the rest of my life without having it happen again.

Then a few months afterwards, Ned and Ashley broke up. Neither of them ever told me and Cara why, but we figured they must have been having problems that we just didn't know anything about. Ned got a different job, and I didn't see much of him. Ashley called Cara a few times, but Cara was still so embarrassed about that incident, that she sort of brushed Ashley off, and they didn't see much of each other either.

Then one day, Ashley phoned me at work. She acted casual at first, and we shot shit for a while, but I could tell there was something on her mind. "Listen," she said at last. "Remember that hot time the four of us had when we played strip poker and then got into a circle jerk?"

"Remember it?" I said. "I'll never forget it. I've been trying to talk my wife into a rematch, but she just isn't having any."

"Well," Ashley said. "I know about a group of people who get together for that sort of thing on a fairly regular basis. They call it a Jack-and-Jill Club. I'd sure like to go, but I have no one to take with me. Do you think you might be interested?"

I was a little hesitant. I'd never cheated on Cara, and I didn't intend to start. On the other hand, maybe this wouldn't actually be cheating. After all, I wouldn't be touching anybody but myself. People might be watching, but nobody else would be touching me. "Yeah, I'm interested," I said at last. "As long as it's just our secret."

"Of course," Ashley said.

I made some excuse to Cara when, about a week later, Ashley and I went to our first Jack-and-Jill Club meeting. It was a blast, even more exciting than that first time, because there were more people in the room, and they were all strangers. Since then, Ashley and I have continued to do it every couple of months. Usually, there are three couples, sometimes four. The people involved never see each other outside the club meetings. It's a great release, and altogether harmless.

Ashley had gotten married. I've never met her husband and I don't think I want to. I don't know what she tells him when she slips out with me for a session of group masturbation, watching and being watched. It's a secret that only she and I share. I don't even feel guilty about it. I'd prefer to do it with my wife, but she just won't go along. That leaves me with no other choice.

8

MONEY MAKES
THE WORLD
GO 'ROUND

SOMETIMES WISDOM CAN BE FOUND IN EVERYDAY expressions. We've all heard someone say, "I've been rich and I've been poor, and rich is better." It doesn't take a degree in economics to recognize that, all other things being equal, life is easier with money than without it. We've also heard it said that money doesn't buy happiness, but it does buy things that make unhappiness a lot easier to live with. This, too, is obviously true.

Although it has been accurately observed that money can't buy love, it has been buying acts of love since the beginning of recorded history. We may turn up our righteous noses at the idea of sex being bought and sold on the open market like any other commodity, but there is no doubt that the purchase of sexual service can solve problems for many people. While this may be especially so of people who are not in relationships, it sometimes applies as well to people who are.

The influence that money has on a sexual encounter varies, depending on the individuals involved and their motivation. This chapter contains stories about two people for whom paid-for sex served two diametrically opposite purposes. Money put Vida in control. It made her the superior participant in a sexual encounter, giving her the right to have expectations without the obligation of fulfilling those of her sex partner. On the other hand, it placed

Ron and his partner on an equal footing, creating a situation in which he did not feel guilt about the acts he wanted to perform.

Many of the people to whom we have spoken described incidents that made us aware of the relationship between money and sex and of the different effects that relationship may have. We have chosen only two of those stories, and two of those effects, for this chapter. Be assured, however, that we have heard about enough such experiences to fill a book. Perhaps we will write it one day.

MASSAGE

At thirty-eight, Vida has dark hair streaked with gray, and her face has developed a series of tiny wrinkles. She is of medium height, with a slight body and narrow shoulders. When she speaks, she has a way of standing that seems to turn her inward, so that one is hardly aware that she has a body at all. Her owlish brown eyes are a window into what is obviously a remarkable mind, but the rings around them show a lack of sleep. She is a microbiologist, highly placed in a major bio-tech firm.

I didn't get to be where I am by slacking. I've worked and studied hard all my life. When I was in school, I put my studies ahead of everything else. I resolved to postpone socializing until after getting my doctorate. I had healthy appetites but allowed myself no real interest in men. For me, there was nothing but books and labs.

Fortunately, my family was well-off, so I didn't have to worry about where the money was coming from. Both my parents are professionals and they encouraged me to spend all my time educating myself. They paid for everything and gave me a handsome allowance besides.

I used to get up at five in the morning and study until classes began around nine or ten. Then, after the day's classes were finished, I'd either spend hours in the labs working on the projects I had undertaken, or I'd return to my room to spend more time with my studies. I finished undergraduate school at the top of my class and completed my master's in two years. Then I went right after the Ph.D.

There were times I was so stressed and tired that I felt like collapsing, but I managed to drive myself on toward my goal. At one point, my body was so fatigued that I thought it could no longer support my brain. Mixed with that, I felt a strong need for sexual release. I had no outlet other than my own fingers and hands, which were not usually very satisfying.

One afternoon, I decided to get a massage. I thought that a good body worker could ease the strain and tension in my muscles. I also thought that I might find the experience stimulating enough to make my subsequent masturbation more successful. For that purpose, I wanted to be sure that the masseur I called would be young, male, and somewhat good-looking.

I asked one of the teaching assistants at the lab if she knew anyone she could recommend. As it happened, she did. I didn't tell her about my specifications, but when she described her masseur, I realized he would fill the bill very nicely. So I decided to give him a try.

I called Alec and made an appointment for him to come to my room with his portable massage table. We agreed on a price of sixty-five dollars for what he termed the "out call." On the phone, his voice sounded strong and even sexy. When he arrived, I was not disappointed. He was in his twenties, powerfully built, with dark wavy hair and bright blue eyes. He was wearing a tank top, and I couldn't help noticing the way the well-developed musculature of his chest and shoulders bulged with strength. His hands and fingers were graceful and the largest I have ever seen.

After setting up his table in my living room, he draped a sheet over it. I asked if he wanted me to pay him in advance, but he shook his head, saying that afterwards would be just fine. He said, "I'll go into the other room while you get undressed. You can leave your underwear on if you'd like, but the massage works out better if you're totally nude. When you're ready, lie facedown on the table and cover yourself with the sheet. I'll come back in as soon as you call me."

As I began undressing, I thought about his words. I needed the massage, but for me this was also supposed to be a somewhat sexual experience. So I didn't really want to leave my underwear on. He had given me the alternatives so matter-of-factly that I didn't feel uncomfortable about being nude. I took everything off. Then, lying on the table as he had instructed and pulling the sheet over me, I called for him to return.

When he came back into the room, he was wearing athletic shorts and no shirt. "All right," he said. "I'm going to use medium pressure. You let me know if you want it lighter or deeper as I go along." He squirted some lotion onto his hands and began massaging my bare feet. It felt surprisingly good. I had been so brain-oriented for most of my life that I was not accustomed to having so much attention paid to my physical self.

His touch was almost loving as he rubbed the soles of my feet with his thumbs and fingertips. Twisting and kneading my flesh, he lulled me into a state of relaxation. Perfect. That was exactly what I had wanted. It felt so good that I drifted into semi-consciousness for a while.

Vaguely, I was aware that he had peeled back the sheet. His hands were moving up and down one of my legs in long sweeping strokes that stopped just short of my groin. With each third up-stroke, his hands moved firmly across my buttock. No man had ever touched me there before. The contact was making me all hot in the crotch.

He continued to work very professionally, probably unaware of the arousing effect it was having on me. When his hands moved over my lower and upper back, trailing over my sides almost to the place where my breasts connected with my body, I heard my-self sigh. He responded by repeating the moves, obviously alert for any sign that he was pleasing his client.

Without the sheet, I enjoyed the feeling of being naked on a table while a man I did not know stroked my skin and kneaded my muscles. Something about the fact that I had hired him and was paying for his attention made it even more pleasing. Rather than feeling vulnerable, I was in control.

When he had finished with the back of my body, I was totally relaxed. In spite of that, however, there was a slight sensation of sexual tension building in my loins. I liked it. I was sure that, later that night, when I lay alone in my bed and reviewed the events of the day, I'd have a fulfilling masturbation session. That's what I was thinking when he asked me to turn over. "I'll redrape you with the sheet if you'd like," he said. "But it will only be coming off again in a moment."

"Then don't bother with it," I replied. I was a little nervous as I turned over. Now my breasts and my pubis would be fully ex-posed to his view. Believe it or not, no man had ever seen that much of me before. Somehow, though, his professional attitude made it all right. Most important, the thought that I was paying for this gave me power and strength.

As I settled down on my back, I closed my eyes, probably from a sense of embarrassment. He went to work right away, stroking my legs, from ankle to upper thigh, again stopping just short of my groin. I could feel myself getting moist. I remember wondering whether he would be able to perceive my excitement. I hoped he wouldn't.

When he finished with my legs, he began rubbing my abdomen, with strokes that went from one flank to the other and back again. His hands came perilously close to the top of my triangle of pubic hair, but never actually came into contact with it. Each time he swept past it, I felt a tingle begin in my vagina and work its way through my whole body.

His hands began moving near my breasts, without touching

them, of course. I felt my nipples hardening to twin peaks of desire. I knew he would see this and wondered what he would think about it. Something inside me wished he would touch them, but he was careful to avoid contact with any of the forbidden zones.

I felt the need to say something about it. "This is my first massage," I said. "I can't control the way my body is reacting."

"Oh, don't worry about that," he answered confidently. "It's a natural response. I'm used to it. You're paying me to be one hundred percent professional. And that's how I'm going to be."

By reminding me that I was paying for his services, he put me back in control and made me feel better about myself. I don't know whether that was what he had in mind, but it worked. I felt my confidence building.

Now, as his hands moved close to my pubic triangle again, I found myself grabbing at them with my own hands and trying to move them lower down on me. "Don't stop there," I said. "Touch me. Go ahead and touch me. I need relief."

"Oh," he said softly. "I couldn't do that. It wouldn't be ethical. It wouldn't be professional. It's not what you're paying me for."

"What if I pay you more?" I asked. "How about another fifty dollars?"

He didn't answer with words. But his hands told me that he was accepting my offer. Gingerly, he began to stroke and pet the hair-covered mound of my pubis. I sighed, certain that release would at last be coming. "You like that?" he whispered.

"Yes," I answered, so softly that I wasn't even sure he could hear me. "I like it. And I need it."

"I can see that," he said. "Don't worry. I understand what you need. I'll give it to you."

His fingertips began nudging the moist lips of my vulva, stroking lightly at first and then building up in pressure until I felt myself opening to him. He slipped a finger inside and moved it in and out slowly and sensuously, turning and twisting at the same time. His finger was so big that as I closed my eyes, I could picture myself being penetrated by a man's penis. My breathing was becoming labored.

Now, as one finger continued moving in and out of me, those of his other hand found my clitoris. It was already swollen and wet, craving touch. He worked it slowly and gently, rubbing it in little circles as my excitement built. It didn't take me long to reach a climax. When I did, I moaned with abandon. I was entitled to this. I was paying for it.

He kept stroking me until we were both sure that I was completely satisfied. Then he patted my abdomen softly and said, "Was that nice?"

"Yes," I answered. "I liked it very much. Will you come back again next week?"

"Of course," Alec said.

After that, he came to my apartment regularly. He would set up his table and leave the room so I could undress in privacy. Then he would give me a wonderful massage. He never neglected a single muscle of my body. When all of me was totally relaxed, he'd finish me with his fingers the way he had done that first time.

Our arrangement continued throughout my educational years. Soon after I received my doctorate, I stopped calling him. I went to work for the company I'm with now. About a year later, I met Gabe, who is one of the company's top executives. His degree is like mine, but he has given up science for business administration. We started going out together. Although he's a couple of years younger than I, we got along famously. Eventually, we were married.

Lovemaking with Gabe is always a long and drawn-out affair. It's good, but sometimes I feel there is just too much in the way of mutual expectation. He is expected to bring me to the stratosphere, and I'm expected to do the same for him. In a way, he even seems to expect my orgasms to be dedicated as monuments to his skills as a lover. Sometimes, sex with Gabe just seems like more trouble than it's worth.

I wasn't sure of what to do about it, until one day I found myself remembering Alec. I wondered if he was still at his old trade and still at his old phone number. So I gave him a call. Yes, he was still available; and yes, he remembered me very well. I made an appointment to see him, only this time I arranged to go to his studio.

I told Gabe that I was feeling stressed and was thinking about getting a massage. He said he thought it was a good idea. So when I went to see Alec, it was with Gabe's complete approval. Of course, he didn't know, and still doesn't know, that I intended to get a little more than an ordinary massage.

Alec's prices are a little higher now, but the service is still the same. I see him about once a week. At this point, it isn't that I need the sexual release, the way I did when I first engaged his services. No, there's something different going on now.

First of all, I like the idea that I am the only one with expectations, and my expectations are simple. I want an orgasm. Just a simple orgasm, with no emotional ties and no psychological baggage. Then, knowing that I'm paying for it and receiving exactly what I'm paying for makes it even more satisfying. I also like the idea that Gabe is aware that I'm seeing Alec, but has no idea of everything I'm seeing him for.

THE FEMINIST

At forty-three, Ron is rather well-known in his field. For this reason, he insisted that we make it clear to our readers that Ron is not his real name. He also asked us not to identify the city in which he lives or the university where he teaches. Ron is a professor of women's studies and a highly respected spokesperson for feminist causes, with several published books to his credit. Physically, he is of short stature, just under five feet six inches. He is slim and wiry, with agile movements and animated facial expressions. A fringe of

*brown hair surrounds his high, shiny scalp. Smiling, he refers to his
baldness as a sign of virility and intelligence. His most outstanding
feature are his eyes, which are of a piercing aquamarine color and
which move quickly from face to face among the people to whom
he is talking.*

I don't really like being called a feminist. That word implies a
philosophy of female superiority, whereas I believe that both
genders are absolutely equal. I tolerate its use only because referring to me as a male feminist helps sell my books. Anyone who
reads one of them knows that I'm an egalitarian more than anything else.

I feel that way about my marriage, too. Nora and I have been
married for thirteen years. She teaches at the same university as
I do, in the history department. Her speciality is the Middle
Ages. She has written extensively about the abuse and domination
of women by men during that period. She's even appeared on a
few TV shows drawing a parallel between gender-oppression then
and now.

Our relationship is as equal as any partnership can possibly be.
We don't have assigned roles in the household. Sometimes I do
the cooking; sometimes she does it. More often, we eat out. We
don't actually take formal turns cleaning the house, but we are
both very much aware of what has to be done. We both go out
of our way to make sure that neither of us does more or less than
the other.

It works out very well in almost every aspect of our married
life. I say "almost" because, to be honest, I do feel a certain lack
in our sexual relationship. Oh, we have plenty of good sex. But
it's not always the kind I'd like to have. I don't feel I can make
any sexual demands on Nora. If there's something she wants to
do, we do it. If she doesn't want to, we both realize it would be
chauvinistic for me to expect it. As a result, I sometimes find
myself going hungry, as it were.

In the beginning, I tried making suggestions. For example, I wanted to try anal sex. I hinted at it for a while, but she never seemed to get my point. Finally, I came right out and asked if she'd be willing. I remember very well how she reacted. It was as if a cold wind had blown in from the Antarctic. "That's disgusting," she said. "What's more, I think that by asking for it, you've shown a tremendous lack of respect for me as a person." She went on to accuse me of macho posturing. After a while, I realized that she was probably right, so I tendered an apology, which she graciously accepted.

On subsequent occasions, I tried proposing other sexual activities that I thought might appeal to me, but with no more success than I had that first time. For example, once I told her I wanted to come by putting my penis between her breasts. Another time, I said I'd like to have her do me anally with a rubber dildo. Both times, she became offended, saying that it was typical of the male ego to try to force such repulsive acts on a submissive female. She wanted me to understand that she wasn't submissive and would not put up with what she called "that macho bullshit."

Naturally, after being put down so harshly, I didn't feel right about making any sexual demands at all. I even started thinking of myself in the terms that she expressed so eloquently when rejecting my suggestions. So I never again requested anything more than the humdrum normal. I decided I'd just have to live without fulfilling all my desires.

Then I discovered Esmeralda. I don't think there really is an Esmeralda, but that's the name of the escort service a colleague told me about. He's a mathematics professor and not the least bit interested in feminism or any other kind of political movement. We play racquetball together sometimes at the school gym in an effort to stay fit.

One afternoon about three years ago, we were talking about sex, the way men do in locker rooms. I mentioned that I thought I was having some kind of midlife crisis, because I just didn't feel sexually satisfied. He laughed and said, "Why don't you give Esmeralda a call."

He told me that he relied on Esmeralda's Escort Service whenever he felt the need for a little sex on the side. He said that with Esmeralda, there was no pretense. The customers all came by personal recommendation from other customers, and everyone understood what was going on. It was a straight commercial transaction, with sex as the commodity being sold.

The women who worked there were examined regularly by board-certified gynecologists. The strictest sanitary conditions were enforced. All customers were required to use condoms. Esmeralda even had a code I could use when I wanted to be specific about the kind of sex I had in mind.

I couldn't believe it was as simple as that, but it was. My colleague called Esmeralda's in my presence, introducing me and then handing me the phone. A sultry-voiced woman at the other end gave me a personal account number, which is like a secret password, and told me to call whenever I was in need of their service.

I did so the following afternoon. My friend had told me that the escorts would only come to a first-class hotel, so I took a room at one of the better places in town and made my call. Giving my personal account number, I used the code expression for anal sex, saying that I was interested in having an escort join me for dinner at a Greek restaurant.

About half an hour later, there was a knock at my hotel room door. When I opened it, there stood one of the most gorgeous women I had ever seen. I'd say she was in her middle twenties. She had beautiful long brown hair and the face of an angel. Although she was dressed in a conservative business suit, it did little to hide her voluptuous curves. If anything, it emphasized the roundness of her backside. It was almost as though Esmeralda had picked out a girl for me with the attribute in which I was most interested at the moment.

"Hi," she said softly. "I'm Liana. So happy to meet you." She stepped into the room, and I closed the door behind her. Then, without any other formality, she began unbuttoning the jacket of her business suit. Within seconds, she was totally nude.

My God, what a body—the kind of body only a young woman can have, the kind you see in magazines and shake your head thinking nobody really is built like that. Her skin was flawless and taut. Her breasts rode high, with sharply pointed pink nipples. They were totally natural, not the work of a plastic surgeon. She had a neatly trimmed triangle of dark brown hair at the base of her abdomen. I was staring at it open-mouthed when she turned slowly in place to show me her glorious bottom. It was full and round, like two distinct melons, with a deep, dark mysterious crack between them.

She let me look at her sweet butt for a minute and then said, "The fee will be five hundred for your special request. Afterwards will be fine." As she spoke, she bent over, pointing her bottom in my direction. Reaching back with her hands, she spread the smooth globes of her buttocks to reveal the hidden valley between them. "You can do whatever you want in there," she said.

She was all business. I didn't even have time to be nervous. As quickly as I could with shaking fingers, I struggled out of my clothes until I was as naked as she. I was already hard as a rock, even aching a little. As I had been instructed, I rolled on the condom I had brought with me. Then I fell to my knees behind her and pressed my face between her cheeks. There was a musty, sexy smell about her.

She moved slightly, caressing me with the soft membranes that surrounded her anus. I had never done anything like this before to any woman. I was so excited that I could feel little drops of semen oozing from the end of my organ. Tentatively, I licked her anus, feeling it squirm at the contact with my tongue. It was hard to believe that this woman whom I had just met was letting me do this to her, something my own wife would never permit. I was in heaven.

I began to feel more confident, driving my tongue in and out of her, getting her anus all wet and lubed. I was thinking of nothing but the instant when I'd be able to thrust my penis into her tight rear opening. I was so eager to do it that I just couldn't wait anymore. I stood and placed my hands on her hips, moving her forward until she was sprawled facedown on the bed.

I climbed onto the bed between her legs and crept toward her. My penis was swinging as I inched my way closer. Its head began grazing her buttocks, first one then the other. Finally I was close enough to place it against her tight anal opening.

"Yes," she murmured. "You can put it right in me there. You can do whatever you want to me there."

Her words of encouragement drove me onward. Humping my hips forward, I buried the tip of my penis in her opening. It was tight, but welcoming. Ever so slowly, I eased myself deeper inside. She assisted me by lifting her hips and raising her bottom toward my thrust. Sounds of pleasure were coming from her throat. "Yes, put it all the way in me," she crooned. "Put it all the way in my ass."

That was all I needed to hear. With one final thrust, I drove it all the way in, until her soft buttocks pressed against my pubic mound. I couldn't believe that my penis was inside this woman's anus. I couldn't believe how good it was, how much in command it made me feel, and how much I liked the sensation.

"I'm yours," she whispered. "Do with me as you like." Her words inflamed me, making me begin the rhythmic in-and-out movements of intercourse. I was in her anus and I was in total control. I wanted to have my orgasm in her there and could think of absolutely no reason why I shouldn't. I kept pumping forward and back, forward and back until it was upon me.

I wanted to be sure she knew it, so I shouted, "I'm coming, Liana. I'm coming in your ass." The sense of freedom I had as I spoke those words and began to climax was unrivaled by any other sensation I had ever known. When it was over, I was filled with gratitude.

We lay there for a while with my softening penis still buried in her anus. As it began to withdraw from the heated temple, her buttocks clutched hungrily at it. She was trying to hold on to me for just a moment longer. Finally, it separated from her. I rolled over onto my side next to her and she turned to kiss me on the lips.

"That was sooo nice," she whispered.

Later, after she had dressed and gone, I lay there alone thinking about the experience. I had gotten exactly what I wanted, yet I didn't feel that I had oppressed a woman or engaged in an unequal relationship. On the contrary, we had been perfect equals, in an arms-length business transaction. I was the customer and she the supplier. Each of us was free to do business or not do business with the other. She wanted to please her customer and even derived satisfaction from doing so—emotional as well as economic satisfaction. I got what I had bargained for.

Paying for sex made me the woman's equal. It gave me the right to be as demanding as I pleased, to do exactly what I wanted to do. I had a perfect right to say I wanted anal sex, without being accused of macho oppression. If the woman wasn't interested in earning a fee that way, she could send in someone who was. The idea of purchase-and-sale allowed me to fulfill my male needs without any false sense of macho superiority.

Since then, I've called Esmeralda's on several occasions. Usually, I use the code to specify the kind of sex I want. Sex between the breasts is called "chicken fricassee." When I request it, they send me a woman with huge soft breasts so that I can get the most out of my desire. When I mention the name "Johnson," they send a woman with a strap-on dildo to do me anally, the way my wife never would.

I'm always satisfied. I've learned something I never knew about myself. Paying for exactly the kind of sex I want makes me feel taller, stronger, more virile, and more in control of my own life. I don't have any guilt about the role played by Esmeralda's escort, because she's an equal partner in the transaction. I don't even feel guilty about being unfaithful to Nora. After all, it's not like I'm having an affair or falling in love with another woman. I'm just buying what she won't give me.

9

LOOK AT ME

EVERYBODY LIKES TO FEEL SPECIAL. VERY FEW EXPERI-
ences convey that feeling as well as being the center of attention.
The knowledge that we are being noticed with approval by others
makes us proud to be who we are. It gives us a sense of being
something more than a nine-digit file number in the social security
system.

This makes every one of us a bit of a showoff. Even those who
are shy or timid look forward to the fifteen minutes of fame promised them by artist Andy Warhol. The limelight is definitely intoxicating.

The streak of exhibitionism that runs through us all does not
necessarily have anything to do with sex. In some people, however,
sex and showing off are inexorably intertwined. Having someone
look at their bodies brings them a sense of erotic excitement unrivaled by any other experience. They are aroused by being seen,
especially unclothed, and by being desired for the way they look.

Sexual exhibitionism may lead to encounters and adventures
that are remembered for life. On the other hand, the thrill of
exposing or exhibiting oneself may be a sexual end in itself. This
chapter contains stories about both kinds of people.

Kristen was an exhibitionist all her life, from gymnastic dem-
onstrations in her childhood to cheerleading in high school and

college. Showing her panties to thousands of horny men brought her into a situation that will titillate her forever. Max is so proud of the size of his genitalia and so fond of showing off that he has turned his exhibitionism into a part-time career. Kristen and Max have something in common beside their desire to be seen by others: the need to keep their spouses from knowing where this desire has led.

CHEERLEADER

Kristen is a bubbly twenty-year-old who could easily pass for an adolescent. She has a childlike way of tossing her long, straight platinum hair and batting her brown eyes while pouting her full lips into an expression that she calls her "spoiled-brat look." She is five-foot-six, with a blossoming body that is tight and perfectly proportioned. Her narrow waist separates her flaring bosom and hips. Her long, shapely legs are well-muscled. Her abdomen is flat, belying the fact that she has recently given birth to a child.

I look pretty good, don't I? Sometimes I just want to thank God for making me so beautiful. My looks have always attracted attention, and I've always known how to make the most of it. I got into college on a cheerleading scholarship. That was before I got pregnant and dropped out, of course.

I started taking gymnastics when I was five. Even back then people would stop and stare at me when I bounced on and off the vaulting horse. In high school, I was head of the cheerleading squad. I was the one who made up the routines and led the other girls through them. It came easy to me. I'm what you might call a natural.

I loved being the center of everything. I knew that when the high school football teams were battling it out, fans were really just waiting for halftime so they could get a look at me leading my girls in the numbers I had choreographed. All eyes would be on me as I jumped high into the air, with my skirts flying every which way. I knew the men in the audience were trying to get a look at my butt. That turned me on, even when I was a kid. I just love showing off.

When I started college and went to my first cheerleading meeting, I looked around the room and knew right away that I was going to be the star, just as I had been up until then. All the girls were pretty, but none of them had what I have. I could feel that special talent working inside me.

The coach was a very masculine-looking woman in her forties. I was shocked when I first saw her. What could she possibly know about pretty young girls like us or about performing the sexy routines that kept the fans in their seats during halftime? She surprised me, though.

All we did at that first meeting was go over the rules and the practice schedule and stuff like that. We received our uniforms, but didn't put them on. As we were wrapping it up, the coach asked me to stay for a moment, saying something about the paperwork for my scholarship. I got a kind of creepy feeling when we were alone in the locker room. She just stood there for a minute, looking me over as if she was appraising some piece of livestock or something.

After a few moments silence, she said, "Kristen, I'm thinking of putting you at the center of the line." I felt myself tingle when I heard that. In cheerleading, the center of the line is the star. She's the one everybody is really looking at; the one who sets the pace for all the other girls. "Do you think you could handle that?" she asked.

"Oh, yes, Coach," I answered. "I was the center on my high school squad. Everybody said I was great at it."

"Yes, you were," she answered. "I saw you work. I was the scout who approved your scholarship."

I hadn't known that. I was a little more impressed with her

now. After all, she knew enough to recognize my talent. "I won't let you down," I said.

"Wait a minute," she responded. "I said I'm thinking about putting you at center. I haven't quite made up my mind yet. I saw you in your high school uniform, but I think I'd better see how you look in ours." I didn't say anything. "Why don't you put it on," she suggested.

"Okay," I answered. I loved wearing a cheerleader's uniform. It's made to show off a girl's best qualities. I knew that once she saw me in it, there'd be no question about that center spot. I picked up the maroon satin top with the school's logo on it and held it in my hand, waiting for her to leave or at least turn her back. I soon realized that she had no intention of doing so.

I hesitated for a moment and then just shrugged. Usually the members of the squad all changed at the same time anyway. Why not? So I just pulled my sweater off over my head and tossed it onto the bench. I could see the coach's eyes boring into me, examining the way I filled my white lace bra. I was conscious of the fact that the dark circles of my nipples were showing through the light material. I could see that it was affecting her. I liked the idea of turning her on, even though she was a woman.

Instead of putting on the cheerleader top right away, I slipped out of my jeans, so that she could look at me in my bra and panties. I was teasing her, I guess, and having a real good time. She said nothing. Finally, moving slowly and sexily, I put on the top. When I picked up the short pleated white skirt and began to step into it, she said, "How about the briefs?"

Usually, cheerleaders wear satin briefs under the skirts. They're kind of like bathing-suit bottoms and part of the outfit. I had always skipped them, so that when I jumped up and down the spectators would be able to see my panties. Usually I wore the skimpiest, most transparent underwear I could find, to be sure everybody got a real good look. That's one of the reasons I was always the center of attention.

"Can't I just wear my panties?" I asked, trying to make my

voice seductive. "I think the men in the audience would prefer that, don't you?"

The coach laughed. "I knew it," she said. "You were made for this. When I watched you at the high school games, I noticed that you weren't using the uniform briefs. I like that. I approve. Let's face it; football is big business for this university. The athletic department doesn't like to admit it, but cheerleaders sell more tickets than quarterbacks. A girl in lace panties is worth a dozen linemen. You go, girl."

I was a little worried that the coach might try something with me. I mean she was so masculine-looking, and all. But she was all business. After she watched me change in and out of my uniform, she told me that I had the center spot. It was quite a feather in my cap, considering I was only a freshman and had just joined the squad.

We practiced every day until the season began. By then we were ready for our debut. The high school stadium had only about a thousand seats, and they were never all filled. But the college stadium held more than twelve thousand people, and most of the time the tickets were completely sold out.

I'll never forget the feeling I had as we went through our routines that first night. I knew that there were thousands of eyes trained on my bare legs and my tush. I knew that college boys and grown men were going blind trying to see through my sheer panties. When I kicked my legs high in the air, I could hear a sigh of desire pass through the audience. It was more exciting than the catcalls and hoots that some of the guys let loose.

Of course, being the center of the line made me the most popular girl on campus. I had tons of dates with the best-looking guys around. You may not believe this, but I was still a virgin at the time. I guess men always found me so attractive that I didn't have to put out the way other girls did. I could have my pick of them without giving anything at all in return.

Then one night, after a game, I met Harry. He greeted me as I was walking out of the locker room, calling me by name. I was a little taken aback because I didn't know him at all. He was old, maybe forty, maybe even older. "Hi, Kristen," he said. "That was some show you put on tonight. I couldn't take my eyes off you."

At first I thought he might be some kind of pervert, the kind that hangs around the locker room hoping for a chance at one of the girls. Then he told me his son was Don, one of the first-string players on the team. I knew Don, though I had never gone out with him. Funny, except for their faces, father and son weren't very much alike. Don was big and brawny, built the way a football player should be. His dad looked like an accountant. Sort of short and a little on the chubby side, with glasses set in black plastic frames. I thought he was cute, though.

"Don's out with the team. Can I give you a lift somewhere?" he asked. "Maybe stop for a drink or something?"

I was just eighteen and not legal for drinking, but I didn't tell him that. I was kind of surprised that a man his age would be interested in me. I mean, I know I'm pretty, but still, I was just a kid. He was a grown man and all. "Sure," I said. "I'd like that."

He took me to a quiet cocktail lounge, quite a distance from the campus. It was nothing like the places where the college kids hung out. This was very sophisticated, with dim lights and little tables. A piano player was tinkling away in the background. The waiter never even carded me, probably because of who I was with. All of the people who worked there called Harry by name.

After a few drinks, I realized I was starting to feel tipsy. Harry must have noticed it, too, because he said, "Well, little girl, I think maybe it's time we left." The way he called me "little girl" sort of thrilled me. It made me feel very secure with this older man.

When we got to his car, he opened the back door for me, instead of the front. I didn't exactly understand, but I went along with it and got in. He slid in beside me. "You're one beautiful girl, Kristen," he said, slipping his arm around my shoulders. "I watched those cheerleading routines of yours and sat there all night with a hard-on. You're really something else." Before I knew it, his lips were against mine.

I had never been kissed that way before. Most of the boys were clumsy about it. Sometimes, their teeth would bump against my lips and hurt me. Harry knew exactly what he was doing. As we kissed, I felt his tongue slide into my mouth. At the same time, his hands began moving all over me.

I was wearing a skirt and sweater. I felt him caressing my breasts under the sweater, boldly and confidently. When the boys did it, there was always an awkwardness about it, as though they were afraid that I would stop them at any minute. Usually I did. Harry took my breasts in his hand like he had a right to them. I couldn't even think of stopping him.

As his other hand went under my skirt, he whispered, "I was staring at your panties all evening from a distance. Now I want to see them close up. He lifted my skirt, exposing my underwear to his view. My head was swirling from the alcohol and from the intoxication of being on exhibit for him. This was even more exciting than displaying myself to the impersonal crowds. Here he was right beside me, looking and touching at the same time.

His fingers traced the curve of my sex right through the crotch of my panties. Before I knew it, he was pulling them off. His hands went to my thighs, spreading them to open my pussy. He stroked me for a few moments and then pulled me up onto his lap. I hadn't noticed before, but his pants were undone and his massive organ was standing straight up from his groin. With expert movements he placed me over him and lowered me into position. I felt him entering me slowly but surely. There was a moment of pain, and then pure pleasure as the thickness of him filled me.

He started kissing me again, his tongue running all over my lips and teeth as he penetrated me. He had lifted my sweater and worked my bra up so that my breasts were free. He held them in his hands, stroking and petting them, turning and twisting my nipples as he drove his giant cock in and out of me. It felt wonderful.

After a few minutes, his breathing got hoarse. He was murmuring things I didn't understand. I may have been inexperienced, but I knew exactly what was happening. He was about to have a climax. Even though I was a bit drunk, I thought about the fact that this was unprotected sex. It felt so good, though, that I just didn't worry about it. When I felt his body pulsing and pumping, I knew he was coming.

He kept it up for a long while. I wondered whether I should act like I was coming too, but I didn't. When he was done, he said, "That was your first time, wasn't it, Kristen?"

I was a little embarrassed, but I nodded my head.

"That's why you didn't have an orgasm," he said. "You will next time. I promise you."

He kept the promise, too, the following week when I met him at the same cocktail lounge. This time, he took me to a motel, where we made love in a bed. I came and came and came.

After my experiences with Harry, I felt different; more like a woman. I continued going out with boys from school, and sometimes I had sex with them. Most were inept compared to Harry, who I still saw occasionally.

When his son Don asked me out, I thought it would be a real hoot to go with him. Maybe we'd end up having sex, and I could compare his technique with his father's. In fact, that's exactly what happened. Don wasn't as good at it as Harry, but he was certainly better than the other boys I was dating. After going out with him a few times, I stopped going out with the other boys all together. When Don and I started getting serious, I even stopped seeing Harry.

Soon after that, though, I discovered that I was pregnant. From the timing, I couldn't be sure whether the father was Harry or Don. Naturally, Don knew nothing about my relationship with his father. So when I told him about the baby, he insisted we get married right away, before I started to show.

We've been married almost two years now. The baby is beautiful. Everybody says he looks like both his dad and his granddad. I still don't know which of them is the father. Maybe it doesn't matter, anyway, since it's all in the family.

I don't really know whether Harry suspects that the baby might be his. He's never said anything at all about it to me. Of course, Don still knows nothing. As far as I'm concerned, it will always be my own personal secret.

MALE STRIPPER

Max, thirty-four, works in a hardware store. He is an absolute Adonis, with thick, wavy ash-blond hair and steel-gray eyes. His tall and powerful body is magnificent, as though sculpted by a master. He wears the briefest possible clothing: a tank cut to reveal the bulging muscles of his shoulders, chest, arms, and back, and athletic shorts that show the tree-like shape of his thighs and the sinuous curves that begin at his ankles and seem to reach all the way to his groin. He is disappointed when we fail to accept his offer to show us his body by removing all of his clothes.

Well, since you won't look for yourselves, you'll just have to take my word for it. I have the longest, fattest cock you've ever seen. Well, I mean, you haven't seen it, but believe you me it's bigger than anything you ever have seen. That's why I love to show it off.

I've been into body-building since I was a kid. It shows, don't it? I've been spending two, three hours at a time in the gym, three, four days a week, just about all my life. See these muscles? Believe you me, that takes work. You don't get those by watching Schwarzenegger movies. I'm not on steroids, either. Believe you me!

When I was a teenager, the girls lined up to go out with me. I took them in turn and I screwed 'em all. They'd see me walking around without a shirt, and that's what would hook them. I'd watch them sneak a peek at my physique. After a while, I'd just offer myself to them, real casual, you know. I'd be all like, "Hey, wanna go out?" I loved watching them melt when I asked them.

I didn't have to spend a lot of money on them or anything. Mostly, take 'em for a pizza or something. Then find a quiet spot where I could let them get a good look at me. Off came the shirt and then the pants. Even with my Jockeys on, they could tell they were in for something special. Finally, when I'd slip my underwear off and this big bopper of mine would come popping out, they'd just sit there stunned, staring at it.

I loved seeing that look on their faces when they got a glimpse of old ironside. It would be a mix of, like, awe and fear. They'd be all like, "Oh, how am I ever going to get that monster in me?" But, believe you me, scared or not, that's just what they wanted. I didn't wanna make it too easy for them. First I'd kind of stall around, you know, making them look at it for a good long while. Then maybe I'd have them suck it. That was something they were usually glad to do, because they figured they'd have to get it good and wet so it would fit.

Finally I'd put it to them. Man, that look of terror that came across their face as I slammed it in there. I'd feel that pussy stretch and pull and get all tight around me. I didn't let nothing stop me. I went for it all. Just keep going until I hit rock bottom. Usually, by then I'd be so turned on by their admiration, I'd just let my juices fly. Didn't matter to me whether they came or not. I don't think it mattered to them either. They were thrilled just to get a piece of my action.

Once the word got around that I was hung better than Johnnie Holmes, I had more girls than I knew what to do with. I never went with any of them more than once or twice. For me, the thrill was that look they got when they first saw old ironside. Just showing them my cock was enough to get me off. I wasn't even all that interested in fucking them. That was more or less something I had to do.

I didn't get married until I was thirty-one. I was having too good of a time. I'm not even sure what possessed me to tie the knot then. Maybe it's just that biological-clock thing. What I think it is, though, is that Rochelle made more of a big deal over my cock than any of the girls I had met before.

We went out on some kind of a date, with both of us knowing that the whole idea was to get alone together somewhere so she could see that cock all her friends had been talking about. Sure enough, after a couple of beers, she brought it up. "I hear you've got a fabulous pecker," she said. "When are you going to show it to me?"

I liked that kind of straight talk, especially when it was about my king-kong dong. "Right now, if you want," I answered, making like I was going to open my fly right there in the bar. She just laughed.

"Tell you what," she said. "My pickup's out in the parking lot, and I've got a camper shell on it. Why don't we go in there?"

Sounded good to me, so I followed her to the truck. As soon as we climbed into her camper, she started pulling at my belt, trying to get me out of my pants as quick as possible. "Come on," she said, sounding like it was real urgent. "I want to see that famous monster."

I was feeling good, so I just grinned and sort of leaned back. "Go ahead," I said. "Do anything you want with me."

I stood there with my hands behind my back, letting her do all the work. She got me out of my pants and undershorts in a hurry, freeing old ironside to stand up straight and sway in the breeze, like. She stepped back and just stared at it. "Oh, my God, Max," she said. "That is the most beautiful thing I've ever seen. Oh, my God, I've just got to kiss it all over."

She dropped to her knees right in front of me and started plastering my dick with kisses, working her way up and down its length. At the bottom, she stopped for a second to lick my balls. Then she went back to kissing my cock. "Mmmm," she moaned. "I've kissed a lot of cocks in my time, but nothing like this one. You're like three men put together. I'm more than impressed."

I liked the idea that she'd been around, that she'd seen other cocks. That meant she could really appreciate the magnificence of mine. Believe you me, she sure did. Pretty soon, she had the head of it in her mouth. Couldn't fit much more than that. She licked and sucked on it like there was no tomorrow. When it was all coated with her spit, she moved back again. "Oh, man," she muttered. "Just let me look at that beauty."

As I watched her admiring it, I guess I fell in love with her. Anyone who could show that much appreciation was my kind of woman. "Do you want me to fuck you?" I asked.

"Yeah," she answered. "In a minute. I'm not finished looking." I think that's what sank the hook. I let her stare at it for a while longer. Then I fucked her. A few months later, I married her.

In the beginning, our marriage was, like, made in heaven. Every night, when I got home from the hardware store, I'd take off my clothes and walk around naked in our apartment. She would watch me, her mouth open in wonder. The sight of her looking at me that way would get me all aroused. That made my big cock get good and hard, and so she'd stare at it even more intently. Sometimes, she'd talk for a long time about how beautiful it looked, how much she loved it, how it turned her on. Sometimes, she'd insist on showering it with kisses, or licking it, or sucking it. She admired the rest of my body too, my rippling muscles, my tight buns, my powerful shoulders. But mostly, she was devoted to my cock.

After she worshiped it for a while, I'd give her a fuck. She'd scream and wail as old ironside plowed into her. It never took her more than a few minutes to come. I liked that too. I didn't have to do much work.

I don't know, though. After about a year, things started to change. She didn't spend so much time talking about my body anymore. She didn't even seem to care all that much about looking at me. Oh, she still was interested in my cock, but all she seemed to want was to get it inside her and get off on it. I started feeling like a dildo with legs.

By this time, I had a second job, part-time at Goldberg's gym, where I had been working out since I was a teenager. I got a kick out of the way the younger guys there would look me over when I lifted weights, but it didn't take the place of admiration from women. I was really starting to miss that.

Then one night, a friend of Abe's—he's the owner of the gym—dropped in to talk to him. I saw Abe pointing to me, and the guy came over. He handed me a card with the words MONTY'S CAFÉ printed on it. "Hi," he said. "I'm Monty Vallee, proprietor of Monty's Café. You've heard of it, I'm sure. The finest male strippers in town."

Actually, I hadn't heard of it and I told him so. "Well," he said. "No matter. I'd like you to come and take a look. You might be interested in working for me. You can make a fortune in tips. Abe says it's all right with him if I steal you away."

I wasn't exactly sure of what he had in mind. When he suggested I get dressed and come with him right then and there, I decided to go along. What the hell. Believe you me, life can be an adventure.

He drove a big black Cadillac, and I followed in my little Honda. He pulled up in front of a nightclub with a big awning outside. I noticed a line of women waiting to get in. Monty waved me on toward the parking lot in the back. By the time I got out of my car, he was waiting there to lead me in through the back door.

Inside, the joint was smoky and loud. There were tiny tables, filled with tons of people, all women. They were drinking and hollering, and everybody seemed to be having a good time. The tables were clustered around a little stage. There was a guy on it, wearing shorts and a tank. He was sort of dancing, gyrating is more like it, to some loud music blasting from the speakers on the wall behind him.

The women in the audience shouted stuff like "Take it off" or "Show us the goodies." When he had stripped down to a teeny-weeny G-string that barely held his cock and balls in place, he started dancing around from table to table. The women were fighting with each other to shove paper money into the G-string. Every now and then I could see one of them manage to get her fingers inside for a little feel of his dick.

"How'd you like to do that kind of work?" Monty asked me. He must have been reading my mind, because that's just what I was thinking. Man, this was right up my alley. The more I saw, the more I liked it. Just the thought of being on that stage, showing myself to all those women, already had me all turned on. I could only imagine how it would be to actually do it. It would be like dying and going to heaven.

"When do I start?" I answered.

Mr. Vallee laughed. "Tonight, if you want to," he said. I was up for it, so we went into his office to talk it over.

He explained that tonight the management would furnish me with an outfit, but in the future I would be expected to provide my own strip clothes. He was only going to pay me six bucks an hour, but he swore that a good dancer would make ten times that in tips. I was a little disappointed when he told me that I couldn't go beyond the G-string, but I could keep it brief enough to show the outline of old ironside, and that ought to bring in the money.

I started that night and I've been dancing there two nights a week ever since. Rochelle thinks I'm still working at Goldberg's gym. I don't have any intention of telling her anything different. Vallee was right about the bulge in my G-string bringing in the bread. Those girls can't wait to stuff dollar bills in there and maybe get a feel. Some of them shove in fives and tens. I make more money in those two nights than I make all week at the hardware store, even when I was adding to that with my job at the gym.

Believe you me, though, it isn't just the dough that keeps me dancing. There is no thrill like the one I get when I pull off my clothes and show my body off to all those chicks. The best part is that, just about every night that I'm working there, there's some woman who wants to see more than I can give her at Monty's Café. They have all kinds of ways of letting me know. Some slip their business cards into my G-string with the cash. Others mouth words like "Meet me later," or something like that. Some manage to find their way backstage past the bouncers and knock on the dressing room door.

I'm easy. I let them seduce me into meeting them wherever they want. Sometimes, it's just the backseat of their car. Sometimes they have an apartment they take me to. I'm usually in a rush, because Rochelle knows what time the gym closes, and I don't want her to get suspicious. But there's always enough time to get out of my clothes and watch their faces light up when they get a look at old ironside.

I let them suck me off, if they want. I even fuck them when they insist on it. But for me the best part is that expression they get when they find out how well hung I am; how big and hard this cock of mine can get. Are you sure you don't want to see it?

10

GAMES

IN HIS FIRST LETTER TO THE CORINTHIANS, PAUL WROTE
that a child thinks like a child, but a man must put aside his
childish ways. This is a true statement, perhaps, but a sad one.
For when we abandon our childish ways, we lose that wonderful
sense of innocence and freedom that made .childhood so exciting
an adventure.

As children, we were quick to play games, falling into the role
of cowboy or nurse or astronaut with no effort at all. One minute
a child can be a monarch, seated on a throne of gold, the next
minute a slave, forced to build pyramids single-handedly. When
we played at these games, we worried about nothing, except
maybe whether the Martians would seize our ice palace before
Tarzan could come and save us.

Grown-ups play games, too. These tend to be regimented, however, with strict rules, the violation of which may be punished by
five minutes in the penalty box or disqualification. A rare few
adults find a way to recapture the joys of childhood by letting their
imaginations lead them into games that they improvise as they go
along.

Since sex is such an important activity, the games these adults
play are likely to involve sexual activity. When partners in a domestic relationship are both inclined to give their erotic imagina-

tions free rein, they may enjoy playing together. But when one is unable to shake off the conservatism that seems to come with maturity, the other may experience the same frustration a child feels when deprived of playtime.

The people whose stories are told in this chapter have introduced a spirit of play into their sex lives. Because their mates were unwilling to join them, they found play partners outside their primary relationships. Because this is likely to be resented by a spouse, they have kept their sex games a secret. As we retell their stories, we get the distinct impression that, for each of them, the play is more important than the sex. See what you think.

NAUGHTY GIRL

Joan is thirty, with black hair that might not be quite so dark if she didn't enhance it with an assist from something that comes in a bottle. Her eyes are a striking emerald green. She is five-foot-nine, and since she is not at all fond of exercise, a little on the plump side. The excess pounds look good on her, though, giving a voluptuous curve to her bosom and softening the lines of her hips. She giggles when she describes herself as a technical writer.

Well, it's not all that technical. You know those toys you buy for your kids that you go nuts trying to put together? I'm the one who writes the frustrating instructions that come with them. No, I don't do it on purpose to confuse you. Actually, we do our best to make it simple. I know it doesn't always seem to work out that way.

Now, my husband, Darren, is a civil engineer. That's really technical. The stuff he works on, I can't even begin to understand. He's with one of the biggest engineering firms in the world. They send him to all kinds of exotic places to manage projects. Sometimes I go with him, but that isn't always convenient. So I end up spending lots of time alone.

I don't really mind it too much. I try to keep up an active social life even when he's not around. He understands completely and even encourages me to go out and have a good time. Of course, he might not be so understanding if he knew what I'm about to tell you. So please be real careful to disguise my identity, just in case he happens to read your book.

I have some friends that I've known since my schooldays, and they invite me to lots of parties. Some of the crowd are coupled up, but there are singles too, so I never feel awkward going to the parties alone. One night, a few years ago, I was invited to one of those get-togethers while Darren was off in the Middle East somewhere, supervising some highway construction.

The gathering was at Elliott's house. He had just gotten through a rather complicated divorce. The party was supposed to be a celebration of his return to freedom.

I was always faithful to Darren, but I like to flirt. So, as usual, I went to the party dressed in my sexiest outfit. I had on a red dress, with a plunging neckline that showed lots of cleavage, and a very short hemline.

The bodice of the dress was cut in a way that prevented me from wearing a bra. It held me in all right, but I knew that when I bent over, anybody who wanted to could get a good look at my breasts, even at my nipples if the angle was right. All I had on underneath was a brief pair of red lace panties. The dress was so short that I knew my underwear would be on view from behind if I should bend forward. Also, when I sat down, people would be able to peek up my legs at them.

All night long, I made full use of the revealing outfit. I was very conscious of the looks I was getting from all the men and even some of the women. It made me feel good to know that I still had it. I might not have been so careless about exhibiting myself if Darren had been there. But, honestly, I had no intention of doing anything wrong.

The party started breaking up a little after midnight. The couples all left, but some of the single women and I stayed behind to help Elliott clean up. Little by little the others drifted off, until Elliott and I were the only ones left.

As we were drying and putting away the last of the cocktail glasses, Elliott turned to me with a frown and said, "Joan, you were a very naughty girl tonight." I was startled by his words and by the unfamiliar facial expression.

"What are you talking about?" I asked in earnest.

"I noticed what you were doing," he said. "Showing your tits and your panties to any man that wanted to see them. That was very naughty. I don't think Darren would have approved. I have half a mind to punish you for it on his behalf."

"Punish me?" I said. "Who do you think you are?" As I spoke, though, I noticed that he had a hard-on pressing against the front of his pants. Something about that made me feel kind of strange. He was turned on, so he was probably just playing around. I giggled.

"You think this is funny?" he said in mock anger. "I think you'd better come over here." Suddenly his voice raised in volume. "At once!"

I was still confused, but I decided to play along. As I walked toward him, he backed into the living room and sat on the edge of the couch. When I was standing in front of him, he grabbed me and pulled me onto him so that I was positioned facedown across his lap.

I felt his stiff cock digging into my belly as his big hands pressed me against him. With a swift movement, he pulled up the short skirt of my dress. I was embarrassed to be in this position, but at the same time, I felt excited to be on display. I knew that my bottom was barely covered by the thin red lace panties I had on. My sense of embarrassment increased as he grabbed the soft material and pulled it up so that it stretched deep into the tight valley between my ass cheeks. I was totally exposed to him now.

I was kind of dazed and didn't know what to expect, when

suddenly I felt his hand strike my bare buttocks. God, he was spanking me. I couldn't believe it. The first blow stung, but the pain did not compare to the humiliation it made me feel. No one had ever spanked me before. No one!

I began kicking my legs in protest, but it got me nowhere. He held me tightly down against his lap and said, "Don't struggle. That will only make it worse. Just take your punishment." With that, his hand whacked me again, this time hurting still more.

I thought about what he said and decided not to put up a fight. After all, he couldn't keep this up forever, and maybe I did deserve a little punishment for the things I had done. Besides, in a peculiar way, it actually felt good.

When the third slap struck, I realized that it was making my bottom very warm. Surprisingly, it was having that effect on my pussy as well. I didn't understand it. Not at all. Then he smacked me again.

He seemed to be alternating, one spank to each cheek. My flesh felt hot and tingly where he had slapped me, but for some weird reason, I was craving more. The next whack came across both cheeks at the same time.

Suddenly he reached under me and thrust his hand inside my panties, probing my tight-lipped opening with his finger. "Ha," he said. "Just as I thought. Your pussy is wet. You're enjoying this. I don't think I'm spanking you hard enough." As he spoke, he slapped me again and again, each spank a little harder than the previous one. Amazingly, the blows were making me wetter and wetter.

I felt completely at his mercy. He was smacking my ass as though he were punishing a naughty little girl, but my response was that of a woman. I was so turned on that I could feel the moisture flowing from me uncontrollably. I realized that I was reaching a point of no return, that if I didn't do something to put a stop to this, my years of fidelity to my husband would be a thing of the past. But I had no power to resist.

Now he was stopping between smacks to fuck me with his finger, running it deep inside my pussy and then withdrawing it to rub the free-flowing juices all over my outer lips. Once he brought his glistening fingertip to my mouth, saying, "Lick this and see what kind of a naughty girl you are." I did as he ordered, astounded by how excited the taste of my own pussy juice made me as I greedily sucked it from his finger.

I wanted more. I would have begged him to continue, except that no begging was required. The strength of his blows was diminishing, but the tingling heat they left behind seemed to intensify. Pulling the panties tight up against my pussy, he started caressing my burning bottom with one hand. After the rough slaps, the softness of his touch aroused me even more.

With a stiffened finger of his free hand, he penetrated my pussy right through the material of my panties, driving the cloth deep inside me, at the same time pulling it snugly against my swollen clit. He moved his finger in little circles while his other hand stroked my ass, until I began to feel an orgasm building. As I screamed with delight, he rubbed my pussy with both hands, working the soaking material of my panties into every crevice and fold of me.

Just as my climax was winding down, I felt his cock swelling and throbbing inside his pants, where it was pressed against me. He grunted as his cum shot from the tip of it to soak the front of his trousers. I could feel it wetting my belly as well. Our cries mingled with desperate gasps for breath.

When we had both come to rest, I rolled off his lap onto my knees on the carpeted floor. He looked down at the wet front of his pants and laughed, long and loud. As I felt the tingling ache in my thoroughly spanked buttocks, I joined him. We laughed together until the tears flowed.

I stood unsteadily, the skirt of my dress all bunched up around my waist. I was about to yank it down into place when he stopped me by reaching out and grabbing the waistband of my soaking panties. "I think I'd better keep these for a souvenir," he said, stripping them off me with an expert sweep of his hand. "I'll sniff them and play with them when you're back home and I'm lying alone in my bed."

He closed his eyes for a long moment and then opened them again to look into mine. "You know," he said softly. "My ex-wife was so straitlaced that I could never get her to go along with playing sex games with me. It's part of the reason we broke up. We were just incompatible. Somewhere in the back of my mind, I've always known you'd be a terrific play partner. Too bad Darren got to you before I did. We'd have made a happy couple."

I didn't know about that, but I did know that our little spanking game had been lots of fun. I also knew that Darren was way too serious for anything like that. I loved him, and I wanted to stay with him, but I felt a little sad at the thought that I'd never be able to have that kind of fun again.

Then I heard myself saying, "We don't have to be a couple to play together every once in a while. I had a real good time. I'd love to do it again. When Darren isn't around, that is."

Elliott laughed. "That's wonderful," he said. "I know lots of other games we can play. I'll leave it up to you. When you're in the mood, you just let me know."

That was the beginning. Since then, I've called Elliott a few times when Darren was out of town. He's always very imaginative and creative. Our sex games are always a turn-on. Maybe sometime I'll tell you about some of the others we've played. We don't do it very often. Just enough to keep my marriage from stagnating the way Elliott's did. It's our little secret.

DOUBLE DARE

At twenty-two, Reid already has a successful business of his own—a computer store in which he sells all the latest hardware and peripherals. He doesn't look much like the typical nerd, however. He is about five feet ten inches tall and a little on the stocky side.

His light brown hair is tied into a ponytail that reaches well past his wide shoulders. His eyes are almost black, flashing with wit and intelligence. He speaks in a loud, friendly voice, with just a trace of British inflection. Although he grew up in the United States, he was born in England.

My wife, Tate, and I have a terrific relationship. Aside from being married, we're good friends. We're both into water sports and cruising around in our WaveRunners. We both get a kick out of watching football games at the local sports bar while sipping a few beers. We're perfectly compatible in every way except one, and that's sex.

The trouble is that I'm a wild and crazy kind of guy, while Tate is a little on the conservative side. Oh, when we're at home alone in bed together, there's just about nothing she won't do. We go down on each other all the time. We do anal sex occasionally. We watch pornos together. We have a rollicking good love life in the privacy of our own home.

On the outside, though, she's the picture of Victorian womanhood. She acts like *sex* is a word she never even heard of. If anyone tells a dirty joke in front of her, she makes a face like she has just been highly insulted. When we're out socially, if the conversation should turn to matters sexual, she's sure to try to change the subject. If that doesn't work, she looks for some reason to leave. She never, I mean never, permits me to show any affection to her in public.

On the other hand, I like to wear my sexuality on my sleeve. I have no objection to having people see me embracing my wife. I'd even like to feel her up now and then in the presence of other people. I tried it once, though, and she made it quite clear there was to be no more of that.

Maybe that's why I spend so much time with Ken and his wife, Eva. Tate and I used to get together with them fairly often. We'd meet at the local pub to watch games on the big screen they have there. We'd laugh, hoist a few, make little bets on the game, and generally have a good time. I thought Tate liked them well enough. Until one evening, her feelings about them changed.

We were sitting at the bar, with more than a few drinks under our belts, when Eva predicted that the kicker would make the extra point. Ken said, "No way." Then he added, "I'll bet you a dare he doesn't."

His wife said, "You're on."

Neither Tate nor I quite understood what the bet was all about, until the kick went astray. Ken pounded his fist onto the bar triumphantly. "I won," he crowed. "You owe me a dare."

"Okay," his wife answered. "What'll it be?"

"I dare you to show your tits to the bartender the next time he fills our glasses," Ken said, snorting with laughter.

I was a little surprised to hear his words. Tate's face registered positive shock. I don't think either of us believed that Ken and Eva were serious. Then the barkeep came around, and Eva surprised us and him as well by reaching down, taking the waistband of her sweater in both hands, and pulling it all the way up to her shoulders. She had nothing underneath it, so her boobs popped right into view.

The bartender was startled at first, but then, affecting the nonchalant attitude for which his profession is known, said, "Thanks for the tip. Same drinks all around?"

I liked getting a look at Eva's boobies. More than that, I liked the free and easy attitude that existed between her and Ken as they played their little dare game. I thought it would be great fun to try it myself. I turned to Tate, who was doing her best to pretend the whole thing had never happened. "Hey," I said. "I'll bet you a dare on the outcome of this quarter."

My wife turned to ice. If looks could kill, I'd be long in the ground by now. "No way in hell," she said, her voice showing a mixture of anger and disgust. "And if you don't mind, I think I want to go home now."

I realized I was in deep water, so I crooned, "Sure, honey. Let's go." I said my good-byes to our friends, while Tate remained stone silent. She kept it up all the way home and well into the following day. When finally she did deign to speak to me again, she made absolutely no mention of the previous night's events.

The following weekend, I expected that we'd be meeting Ken and Eva at the sports bar again, as we usually did during the football season. I was not too surprised, however, when my wife announced that she was not going. "I don't think I enjoy their company any more," was all she would say.

"Well," I responded in frustration. "I don't intend to spend the weekend sitting around the house."

"I'm not asking you to," she answered. "Why don't *you* meet them. Go ahead. Have a good time. I won't mind. Really, I won't."

You know, women have a way of saying one thing when they mean another. So I really was not sure whether she was serious or not about my going myself. Nevertheless, I decided to put her to the test. My brain may have been counseling against it, but my feelings were driving me on. "All right," I said. "I will."

When I got to the bar, Ken and Eva were sitting at a table, obviously waiting for Tate and me. They expressed a bit of surprise when I told them Tate wasn't coming. I didn't see any reason to say why, so I just mumbled something about her having a head-ache. We ordered drinks and settled down to watch the game.

At one point, Ken and his wife got into a disagreement about who would be brought in to replace a player injured on the field. When Ken insisted he was right, Eva said, "Okay, I'll bet you a dare." Her words excited me. This was going to be another fun evening.

When it turned out that Ken was wrong, I was curious to see what his wife had in mind for him. "All right," she said. "Here's the dare. You go into the men's room and take off all your clothes. Then come running out, making one full circuit of the room before going back and getting dressed again."

Without a word, Ken went off to comply. I thought this was a bit radical and would get us thrown out of the bar for sure. But when he came running out of the lavatory, stark naked, everybody in the place just whooped and hollered, accompanying his circuit with raucous laughter. A few moments later, he was back at the table fully dressed and holding a beer in his hand as if nothing had happened.

By now, the game was practically over. The score was close. Eva asked me which team I favored. When I picked the one I thought was going to win, she said, "Would you bet a dare on that?"

The idea appealed to me. I immediately began thinking of the sexy things I could make her do. "It's a bet," I said.

When the game ended, my team was six points behind. I found myself becoming a little nervous in an excited kind of way. What would she make me do? Whatever it was, I knew it would be a little embarrassing, and a little arousing as well. I was surprised when Ken said, "Game's over. Let's get out of here."

When we got to their car, Eva slid in behind the wheel and said, "Let's go to the Stop'n'Shop and pick up a six-pack." Then she giggled and added, "Reid will go in and buy it—wearing nothing but his shirt."

The shirt I had on reached to just below my hips. I knew that if I stood perfectly still, it would cover me, but of course that would be impossible when I walked in and went to the cooler to pick out a six-pack. Still, the thought of doing it was exciting and challenging.

"I'll bet he does it," Ken said. "Our boy is as game as they come."

"I don't think so," his wife answered. "I'll bet he chickens out."

"Okay," Ken said. "Let's bet a dare on that one."

"You're on," Eva said, as she guided the car into the parking lot of the convenience store.

We sat there for a moment as I mustered the courage to perform the dare. Then, to Eva's surprise, I slipped out of my trousers and shorts. I was in the backseat, and Eva made no bones about turning around to watch me. Sitting there and struggling with my clothes, I knew my private parts were exposed to her view. She looked at them without any pretense.

"Nice," she said. "But are you going to go in there like that?" Rising to the challenge, I stepped out of the car and walked boldly into the shop. Without looking about me, I went straight to the cooler, selected a six-pack of beer, and carried it to the checkout counter.

I was vaguely conscious that my privates were showing below my shirttail, but the guy behind the counter acted as if nothing strange was happening. I could see two teenaged girls standing off to one side giggling and pointing. Far from bothering me, that actually turned me on. When I returned to the car, I made sure to turn toward them so that they could get a good look.

Slipping into the backseat of the car, I tossed the beers to Eva and said, "Well, I didn't chicken out, did I?"

Ken laughed. "You sure didn't," he said. "Now Eva owes me a dare. Reid, what do you think we should have her do?"

I had a million ideas, but didn't have the nerve to express any of them. "I'll leave that to you," I said. "After all, she's your wife and it was your bet."

"Well," he began. "You won the bet for me, so I think I'll dare her to give you a blowjob. Right here in the parking lot. What about that, Eva? I double dare you."

I was astounded. I never thought my friend would be that free with his wife's favors. I was excited by the idea of having her perform oral sex on me, but even more turned on by the surroundings and the game-like atmosphere.

"Sure," she said casually. "I'll do it. I'll even admit that after seeing that equipment, I'm kind of looking forward to it." She climbed over the front seat and joined me in the back. We were parked under a lamppost and the light was illuminating the interior of the car. All three of us were aware that anyone who passed would be able to see everything that was going on.

That didn't stop Eva, though. With relish, she bent over me and took my penis in her mouth. The weird combination of factors and events had raised me to peak erection. The touch of her lips and tongue against my stimulated organ sent a shudder through my body. I looked up to see Ken watching intently as his wife began moving her head up and down over my swollen member. He appeared to be enjoying himself.

With him watching, however, I wasn't sure about how I should react. Should I play it for fun, strictly a dare? Or should I let myself go and give in to the sexual feelings that her oral ministrations were bringing to me? I'll admit that if I had to resolve that dilemma with my mind, I would probably still be struggling with it. But my body took over and I just let the wonderful feeling pass over me.

Eva was quite expert with her mouth. She sucked lightly while swirling her tongue all over me. She was making a humming sound deep in her throat, and the vibrations were increasing the pleasure. It was obvious that she was enjoying the task as much as the rest of us.

I realized I was about to climax and felt highly unsure of how to handle it. I wondered if I should tell her so she could have the opportunity of taking her mouth away. Yet how could I say "I'm going to come" in front of her husband, who also happened to be my friend? Again, the problem was solved by the natural functions of my body.

Without the aid of thought, I began to ejaculate, exploding into her sucking mouth while her husband watched with an expression of glee playing over his face. The more I came, the harder she sucked, as though trying to drain me of every possible drop in fulfilling Ken's dare. When I was done, I felt her licking me clean.

Suddenly a pair of headlights shone into the car as a highway patrol vehicle pulled into the parking lot only a short distance from us. Ken started laughing. "They must be on a doughnut run," he said.

As if to prove him correct, the officers got out of their vehicle and headed straight for the store without even noticing the aberrant sexual behavior taking place right next to them. Eva joined her husband in laughing. Pretty soon the three of us were half hysterical with mirth.

When I arrived at home a little later on, my wife asked, quite civilly, "Did you have a good time with your friends?"

"It was okay," I answered, gloating inwardly on what a really fine evening it had been.

"The game ended an hour and a half ago," she said. "Did you do anything afterwards?"

"Yes," I answered. "Eva wanted to eat something, so we went to the convenience store and sat in the parking lot for a while."

Tate is still unwilling to join Ken and Eva for evenings out, so I meet up with them myself every once in awhile. I'm quite impressed at how open the two of them are. For example, on one recent outing, I lost a bet and Ken dared me to have sexual intercourse with his wife under a blanket in the park, while there were picnickers all about us. As before, he seemed to enjoy watching. The sex was nice, but the excitement really came from performing the dare more than the physical contact.

I'm still amazed at the ideas the two of them come up with. They never seem to run out of dares for me and for each other. I absolutely love the sex games we play together and don't want to give them up. I wish my wife would join in, but since she isn't willing, I'll just have to keep the fun to myself.

11

THE SPICE OF LIFE

WE ALL KNOW THAT VARIETY IS THE SPICE OF LIFE. British statesman Benjamin Disraeli added that it is the mother of enjoyment. Even the most passionate chocolate lover orders pistachio ice cream occasionally, if only for the novelty of tasting a different flavor.

For many people, the same is true of sex. In *The King and I,* the king explains to the English governess he has hired that a man is like a bee, which goes from blossom to blossom to blossom. On the other hand, he says, a woman is a blossom, which does not go from bee to bee to bee. Of course, the king was wrong about botany as well as human nature. Any flower may be visited by many bees, just as any woman may feel the need for many sexual partners.

This chapter tells the stories of people who engage in promiscuous sex primarily because they seek variety. Francine blames the urge on her husband, who she says is older than she and does not offer much in the way of sexual satisfaction. Jim complains that sex with his wife has become too predictable, that they always make love according to the same pattern.

In explaining the reasons for their infidelity, we do not believe that they are being completely honest with themselves. After all, if an unsatisfying sex life is the only thing compelling Francine to seek an extramarital mate, why does she keep four lovers at a time and arrange to change them every six months? If Jim's sole interest is in breaking out of the sexual routine into which he and his wife have fallen, why doesn't he try to do something about it in his own marital bedroom or seek a single outside partner with a larger erotic repertoire than his wife's? We do not say this to be critical of their, or of anyone else's, chosen lifestyle. We simply recognize that what is truly driving them, just as it drives so many others, may simply be the desire for sexual variety.

CAMPUS RENTALS

Francine is twenty-four, with an exotic look that comes from her mixed ethnic background. Her Vietnamese mother married her American father during the war, when he was stationed in Saigon. Francine is petite, standing just short of five feet, with a heart-shaped face, long glossy black hair, and dark almond-shaped eyes, all inherited from her mother. But her innocent-looking smile is right out Middle America. Her skin is a creamy tan color and appears soft and smooth.

My parents have both passed away. My mother taught me I should always have something of my own. Even though my dad took good care of her, she worked hard to acquire something of value that she could leave me. She always said that the one thing that would last forever was real estate. So she scrimped and saved until she had enough for a down payment on a big old house near the university campus. She divided it up into four efficiency studios and rented them out to college students, taking in enough to pay the mortgage, with a little profit for herself. I was their only child, so when they died, it passed to me.

I got married kind of young. My husband, Floyd, is twenty-five years older than I am. He's a wonderful man, and I like him very much. But I can't really say that I married him for love. He's very good to me. He is very successful financially, and that's important too. We live in a beautiful house, with a full-time live-in maid. He gives me everything I need or want.

I pay a price for all that, though. He's always busy working or traveling on business. We spend very little time together. It's a good thing that I have my own little enterprise, or I'd have too much time on my hands. My mother taught me right when she said I should have something of my own.

At first Floyd objected to my soiling my hands with the ins and outs of running four rental units. But I stood my ground and eventually he came to understand how important it is to me. Of course, he doesn't know all the reasons why it's so important.

I'm young and vital. Sex is very important to me. I require a lot of it. I have a right to expect it to be satisfying. Unfortunately, Floyd's sexual peak is behind him. Maybe he used it all up on his first wife; I don't know. I do know that on the rare occasions when he tries to make love to me, I always end up disappointed. He huffs and puffs a lot, but mostly all he does is stick it in me and pump a few times before it's all over. He moans and groans, and he expects the same from me. So I give it to him.

The truth is that he has never once given me an orgasm. Well, he gives me everything else I need, so I guess I shouldn't complain. Besides, I'll get along fine, as long as I have the campus rentals.

You see, I rent out the efficiencies on a short-term basis, one semester at a time, so there is always a turnover of residents. I rent only to males. I interview each of them before renting, so I get a chance to pick out the ones who look the sexiest. I think I've developed the ability to guess pretty accurately about whether a young man will be a good sex partner. I'm rarely wrong.

I choose men who are a few years younger than I, to be sure they're in their sexual prime. Being slightly older and being the landlady gives me a certain sense of power over them, so I never have to worry about unpleasant repercussions. I make it pretty clear that I won't rent to the same person two semesters in a row. That way I'm sure that nothing will ever get serious, that my relationships with them will never involve anything more than good, clean, meaningless sex.

When the semester begins and the new crop of tenants moves in, I find lots of work to do in and around the house. I weed the garden. I sweep the hallways. I change lightbulbs in the common areas.

I like to wear a short skirt and tight sweater, both of fairly thin material. I'm small-breasted, so I can get away without a bra. As I work, I think about the pleasures that lie ahead. That makes my nipples hard. I know that the sight of them pressing against the sweater will have the right effect on the college boys who have just moved in.

Lots of times, I go without panties, too. Then, when I climb a ladder to change a lightbulb or to clean the moldings near the ceilings, they can get a peek up my skirt and see my bare ass, or maybe get a glimpse of my full bush. After a few days of that, I can take my pick.

I haven't had a renter yet who didn't come on to me at some point. I may play hard to get for a while, but of course it's what I've been waiting for all along. Before long, I'm managing to have sex with all four of them. I never mention the fact that I'm married, and none of them has my home address or phone number. I'm sure they talk among themselves and eventually find out that I'm doing them all, but that never seems to discourage any of them.

To me there's something very exciting about going into one of the apartment to spend an hour or two making love, knowing that the other men in the building are very much aware of what's going on in there and aware that they'll be getting a turn before long. The young men all seem to be able to get me off, and when I come, I like to make a lot of noise about it. Maybe it's because I have to pretend with Floyd, but when I have a genuine climax, there's no pretending. I just let my voice do whatever it wants. If the other residents hear me, so much the better. It will keep them hot and horny for me until I can get around to them.

At the moment, I have one tenant who is kind of special. He's a big black athlete—a basketball player—and I just get the chills thinking about him. His cock is so big that the first time I saw it, I didn't know how it would fit inside me. But it did.

I had been teasing him for a while: bending over so he could look down the front of my sweater, crossing my legs so that he could peek up my skirt, shaking my little Asian ass whenever he was standing behind me. One afternoon, while I was busying myself around the house, he asked me to step into his apartment, saying he had something to show me. I knew what he had in mind, of course, but I played it all sweet and innocent.

As soon as I followed him inside, he closed the door behind me and took me in his powerful arms. I didn't even pretend to resist. When he started kissing me, I kissed back, passionately. Within seconds, his big muscular hands were moving over my body, stroking my hips and spreading across my back, before cupping and petting my breasts through the material of my sweater. I sighed, to let him know that I was ready for whatever he wanted to do.

Instantly, he slipped his hands inside my sweater. His exploring fingers found my nipples, which were already swollen into erection. He began rolling and tweaking them. I remained passive for only a moment, and then I ran my hands over the bulging muscles of his back and shoulders. I gasped when he stripped the sweater from me and began sucking one of my nipples. In spite of his obvious strength and power, he nursed so gently that it felt like silky threads tickling my most sensitive spot.

He switched from one nipple to the other, licking and sucking and rolling his tongue over my trembling flesh, while his fingers fumbled awkwardly with the clasp at the waistband of my skirt. I was becoming impatient, so I helped him by undoing the clip myself and letting the skirt slide down over my hips and legs. Now I was naked.

I find it exciting to be with a man who is huge and massive. Maybe it's because I'm so little. I also find it exciting to be naked with a man who is still fully dressed. Although I know I'm in control, for a moment, it makes me feel wonderfully vulnerable.

I basked in that feeling for what seemed like a long time. It was probably only an instant. Then I found myself wanting to see him nude and to feel his bare skin against mine. I reached for the buckle of his belt and started working it open. This turned him on so much that I could feel him shaking.

I unhooked his pants and pulled down the zipper of his fly. I struggled to work the pants down over his hips and then shoved them farther until they were tangled around his ankles. I could see his erection straining against the white briefs he had on. There was a little wet spot where the cotton material stretched taut over the tip of his cock. I couldn't wait any longer. Gasping, I reached inside the underpants and took hold of his organ. God, it was huge.

With trembling hands, he pulled and tugged at his garments until he was as naked as I. I stared, goggle-eyed, at his penis. It was the biggest I had ever seen in my life. So thick and long. I could see veins curling their way from base to tip. They seemed to throb against the thin layer of skin that covered them.

Falling to my knees, I tried to take the massive head into my mouth. He was so tall that I found myself stretching my neck all the way back while I pulled downward against his cock's natural tendency to point upward. I did manage to lick the tip with a broad stroke of my tongue, but it felt awkward. In desperation, I pulled him down to the floor and lay beside him, turning so that my head was next to his groin.

As I pressed my mouth to his cock, he began licking my tight pussy. I groaned, even louder than he, when the tip of his tongue penetrated me, forcing the lips of my opening to spread wide for him. His cock was too big for me to suck deep, so I began running my pursed lips up and down its length without actually taking it inside my mouth. Each time I reached the head, I ran my tongue around it in sensuous circles, tasting the salty tang of the fluid that oozed from its winking eye.

I wanted it inside my pussy, but I couldn't really believe it would fit. He was soooo big, and I'm so small. I was afraid that if he climbed on top of me and tried to penetrate me, he would split me apart; I would lose control. But the idea of this huge thing going inside me had me so excited that I was flowing with soft, thick, syrupy fluid.

Using my hands to roll him onto his back, I mounted him. First, I straddled his hips on my knees, letting the tip of his swollen erection graze the opening of my sex. Then, very slowly, I reached down and placed the head of his huge cock between the lips of my flowering vagina. I felt my pussy kissing him, opening itself to invite him in. As if he sensed my dilemma, he remained perfectly still, leaving everything to me.

An inch at a time, I lowered myself down onto him, feeling the exquisite sensation of pleasure-pain as my membranes rolled back to receive him. It seemed that there was no end to the long, slow penetration. His penis went on forever. As I worked it in deeper and deeper, I stared into his face, seeing the expression of ecstasy flood his features. I knew that the fit was tight and that his cock was getting a fine massage from my little Vietnamese pussy.

I don't know how it happened, but eventually I drove it to rock bottom. I could feel the thick curling hairs around the base of his cock tickling the open lips of my vulva and the hardness of his pubic bone pressing against my clit. A rush seemed to flow within me. My body was pouring more and more lubrication to ease his movement inside me. When he was in as far as it could go, I began to rock my body slowly up and down, moaning as the friction brought me one burst after another of sexual pleasure.

Taking my cue, he began to raise and lower his hips, synchronizing his movements with mine, so that he was driving in and out of me like a piston. Each time he plunged to the hilt, he groaned, a guttural masculine sound from somewhere deep inside his throat. As he slowly withdrew, his face took on a look of tension, as though he feared losing his grip on a new world of sexual fulfillment. The stiffness of his lips relaxed again as he plunged up to drive at my core.

I felt an orgasm coming on. I don't usually come that quickly. It was hard to believe that it could be happening so fast. I never even had a chance to think about it. A few more strokes and the whole cosmos turned into a rocket exploding in front of my eyes. The air seemed to fill with vibrant colors as I shouted the joy of my climax.

He kept driving and jabbing with his cock until I finished coming and was ebbing slowly back to the realities of earth. Then, certain that I was satisfied, he let go and began shooting his hot sperm into me. I felt his massive cock growing larger and thicker as it set up for each squirting spasm. I saw his whole body twitching as he delivered his load deep inside my belly.

When he was done, I lay on top of him, listening to the strained sound of his breathing. For the longest time, he panted and sobbed, as though he were gasping out a final breath. Then, little by little, his respiration normalized. He surprised me by wrapping his arms around me and kissing me deeply on the mouth. I felt his tongue sweeping over my teeth and gums, in a gesture that most men perform only as an act of foreplay. I was touched by his tenderness after the sex was over.

It's good to know that I'll have my black lover to please me for the rest of the semester. Of course, I won't neglect the other tenants. And I'll still be looking forward to next semester, when I'll start interviewing my next crop of lovers. After all, variety is the spice that makes the meal of life more satisfying.

Recently, after an afternoon with my basketball player, I came home to find Floyd returned from a business trip and in an amorous mood. I lay back to let him do what he wanted, knowing that I was still filled with semen from my earlier escapade. Somehow, the idea made it a little easier to accept my husband's ineptitude. I suppose that's a benefit that he derives, without knowing it, from my campus rentals.

DOG HANDLER

Jim, thirty-two, is a successful freelance writer. He has contributed chapters to several books about dogs, and his articles on many different subjects appear regularly in some of the country's most popular magazines. He is just over six feet tall and of medium build, weighing in at about 180 pounds. His shaggy red hair has a tendency to fall in front of his freckled face. He seems constantly to be pushing it back. His brown eyes peer at us through thick glasses in frames that are held together at the bridge of the nose with adhesive tape.

Sexual variety was always a theme in my life. Until I got married, that is. I was kind of like the stud dogs I handle—ready, willing, and able to mount and breed just about any female who would let me. I've been training show dogs since I was a teenager. That's about the same time I discovered the pleasures of sex.

You may not be aware of it, but there's a huge subculture out there devoted to breeding and showing good-quality dogs. Some people spend their whole lives traveling around the country, from dog show to dog show. They accumulate ribbons, which are supposed to make their animals more valuable for breeding. Most people really do it for the fun, the thrill of competition, the satisfaction of winning. Another important part of it is the interaction with other dog people. Breeders get to know one another at these shows. That makes it possible for them to find a greater variety of mates for their show dogs.

Somehow, the search for breeding partners seems to carry over into the sex lives of many of the people involved. I found that out the first time I went to a show alone. I had gotten my dog handler's license at around the same time I got my driver's license. My parents, who were also into showing dogs, let me borrow the family motor home to attend a show in another state. Typically, the big shows last a whole weekend. Registration is on Friday evening.

There are events all day Saturday, leading up to the final competition on Sunday afternoon.

I had been to shows before, but always with my parents and their dogs. This time, I was completely on my own, showing a male Irish setter named Muldoon that I had bred and raised myself. Setters have always been my breed.

A little while after I checked in, I was working my dog near my motor home, in the area the show authorities had set up for that purpose. I noticed a woman watching me. She looked to be about ten years older than I was, so I was kind of expecting her to offer some matronly advice. I was a bit surprised when she walked up to me and said, "I think I see a couple of fine studs here."

I was confused and looked around to see what other dog she might be referring to. Mine was the only one around. "I think Muldoon is going to be great some day," I answered. "Which other one do you mean?"

"I meant you," she said, looking me straight in the eye. A few minutes later, Muldoon was safely in my motor home, and I was in hers. She was the one who took my virginity, and I'll never forget her. She taught me things about myself that I didn't know before. I learned things about women's bodies that I still use today. All in all, it was the most educational weekend I ever spent. Muldoon got a blue ribbon, but that seemed unimportant in comparison to what I received.

I had a similar experience almost every time I went to a show. I don't mean educational; I mean sexual. I'm not saying all dog breeders are out there for the sex. It just seems there are lots of women who take advantage of the weekends alone to have erotic adventures. I managed to find them, so maybe it's just something about me.

Anyway, my dogs were doing well. I was doing even better. I went to shows as often as I could, filling my young world with a multitude of sex partners. I increased my stable of dogs, until I had four or five that I was showing regularly. Meanwhile, I was writing articles for dog magazines.

After a while, I started branching out and writing for other kinds of magazines as well. Pretty soon, I had a nice little career going. Best of all, it let me create my own schedule, so I still had time for all the shows I wanted and all that wonderful weekend sex.

They say you can't serve two masters, and it's true. As time went on, I had more and more writing commitments and less and less time for my dogs. After a while, I was down to two, then one. Before too long, I was so busy writing and meeting with publishers that I wasn't going to shows at all anymore. I missed the erotic opportunities, but I was so wrapped up in my career that it didn't seem all that bad.

That's when I happened to meet Veronica. She was an editor working for a magazine that regularly bought my stuff. She called me one day to ask questions about some material I had submitted. We decided to talk about it over lunch. It was what they call love at first sight. We spent about three minutes discussing the article and the rest of the time talking about each other.

Veronica had absolutely no interest in dogs, but that made no difference. We seemed to have lots of other interests in common. Soon we were dating, and soon after that, we moved in together. We had good sex, right from the start. Veronica and I would engage in foreplay for a long time before getting down to the final act. Then it was always long and sweet. I thought I had found the perfect partner.

We got married after a while, and the sex was still terrific. Once in a while, though, I had the feeling that something was missing. I couldn't put my finger on it. There just seemed to be a nagging lack in my life.

I thought maybe I needed to have a dog again. Veronica objected at first. The fact is, she really doesn't care that much for dogs. I held fast, saying that it was important to me. I'd always been a dog person. Besides, I was home writing all day, while she was off at the office. A dog would be good company for me.

Naturally, I got a setter—not just any old dog, but the absolute best I could find. Even though I had no intention of showing him, I still had my standards. I named him Reilly, and we were pals right from the start. In the afternoons, I'd take him to the park and we'd have great times. But it didn't satisfy that nagging need that had prompted me to buy him. I still couldn't figure out what that was.

One night when Veronica and I were making love, it came to me. We started, as usual, by taking off all of our clothes and lying down side by side in bed. Then, as usual, I stroked her breasts until her nipples were hard. Then, as usual, I began licking and sucking them. After that, as usual, I let my tongue travel over her smooth, white belly to her patch of dark pubic hair and started licking her sex. As usual, this brought her to the edge of orgasm. Then, as usual, I mounted her and thrusted until we came pretty much together. When it was done, as usual, we lay side by side in silence.

That was when I realized what the problem was. There was no variety in our life. Everything went according to Hoyle, following some pre-established plan. No surprises. No novelty. Nothing out of the ordinary. What was missing in my life was the sexual variety that came from finding a different sex partner every time I went to one of those weekend dog shows. I didn't realize it, but a resolution to bring that variety back again was already forming inside my subconscious mind.

Consciously, I told myself that it was out of the question. I was a married man now. That meant those days of loose and promiscuous sex were over. I would just have to fill the void with renewed attention to my hobby. I would show Reilly to see how he would place against other dogs of his breed. If he took any ribbons, maybe I'd get a few more dogs and get into breeding again to take my mind off my frustration. At least, that's what I told myself.

I even asked Veronica to join me in taking Reilly to a show. I was not surprised when she turned me down. She had a dozen reasons: She was too busy. She didn't like sleeping in a motor home. She wasn't all that crazy about dogs. She'd find the show boring. And so on. I wasn't really disappointed, though, when she encouraged me to go by myself. I made arrangements to rent a motor home and entered Reilly in a show taking place two weeks in the future.

I spent the time in between working with him, getting him groomed and ready for the ring. I had already taught him all the basic moves, but he had never been in a competition before, and I didn't want to make a total fool of myself. When the big weekend arrived, he was prepared to make at least a decent showing.

I checked in with show officials on Friday night. Saturday morning, I put Reilly through his paces in the first event. I felt a little like a duck out of water, unacquainted with the other handlers in the ring. Then I saw a familiar face. It was Winnie, a woman I had known from the old days. She and I had a few sexual encounters back then. She looked older, but still had a certain aura of raw sexuality about her, maybe because of the memories I had of our coupling.

Winnie's dog won that competition. Reilly didn't even place. Afterward, I went up to her to offer congratulations. She looked at me for a moment without showing any sign of recognition. Then, squinting a bit, she said, "Excuse me, I don't have my glasses on. It's Jim, isn't it?"

We chatted for a while, renewing our friendship and bringing each other up to date on our individual lives. Like me, she was married to someone who had no interest in dogs. After a while, she invited me to her trailer for a drink.

The first drink led to a second, and the second led us to the bed. As I undressed her, it felt like the first time all over again. I had no idea what she would look like under her clothes. I didn't know how she would react to my touch. I couldn't imagine how she would behave when she had an orgasm.

That's what made it exciting. The sense of sexual adventure was returning. I had feelings I hadn't known in years, not since Veronica and I got married. I rolled with Winnie on the narrow trailer bed, thrusting myself into her until we were both satisfied. Afterward, we kissed long and hard.

"Whew," I muttered. "I missed that." I don't imagine Winnie had any idea of what I was talking about, but that was all right.

A few weeks later, I took Reilly to another show. This time, he won a third in one of the events. Again, I saw a woman I had known in the old days. Again, I ended up having sex with her.

At the third show, I hooked up with a woman I had never met before. That was even more exciting, because the experience was a totally new one. She turned out to be a screamer. When she came, she made more noise than a whole kennel full of hounds. I've met and mounted many women since then. I'm loving every minute of it.

Veronica has no objection whatsoever to my renewed interest in dogs. When I show her the ribbons Reilly occasionally takes, she smiles politely, with no real concern. Although she doesn't really understand my attachment to show dogs, she understands that I need a hobby. She says that she thinks it's good for me.

It is a wonderful hobby. Not so much the showing of dogs, but the sexual diversity that it gives me an opportunity to experience. Honestly, a hobby is all that it is. There's no danger of my becoming involved with any of the women I have sex with. The only times I ever see them is at the shows. Mating with them fills a need that I have for a multiplicity of partners.

I realize that I'm still relatively young and hungry, and that it can't go on forever. A time will come when I settle down and become content with a single sex partner. When that happens, Veronica will certainly fill the bill. Until then, I'm making hay while the sun shines.

12

CHAMPIONS

EVERY FOUR YEARS THE WORLD'S GREATEST ATHLETES gather to compete in a series of events known as the Olympics. In doing so, they continue a tradition that began some twenty-eight hundred years ago in ancient Greece. The winners receive gold medals to wear on ribbons around their necks, but their real motivation is to be crowned as champions in their particular sport.

To be a champion is to be recognized as a superior person. There are champion runners, champion heart surgeons, champion investors, champion ballerinas. These are the people who excel, the people to whom all others in their fields look up with admiration.

Although they don't receive the same degree of world recognition, there are some who delight in being sexual champions. To them, the thrill of being dubbed erotic experts surpasses all the other satisfactions of sexuality. They live to give pleasure to others, not necessarily because they are unselfish, but because they can thus prove their abilities and receive the kudos they crave.

Peter, whose story is told in this chapter, admits that he deliberately set out to acquire sexual skill to make up for his unimpressive physique. He selected his mate because she recognized and lauded his prowess more than any of his other sex partners had done. When the routine of parenthood began to dampen these plaudits, he searched for someone outside his marriage on whom he could demonstrate his expertise.

Meg was acknowledged as a sex goddess in her circle of friends. When the glitz of her jet-set life began to lose its glamour, she married an ambitious but conventional politician on his way up. Although she liked living the life of a successful public leader's wife, she found herself longing for her days as an erotic champion. This longing led her to reunite with old friends and pick up the old way of life.

Peter and Meg are trying to live in two worlds. In one, they are gold-medal winners in the sexual arena, recognized as champions in the erotic arts. In the other, they lead an ordinary existence, having ordinary sex like other mortals. Their spouses know about the latter aspect of their lives. Only we know their secret.

CONQUEROR

At first glance, Peter, forty-two, appears somewhat nondescript. He is five feet eight inches tall and probably weighs no more than 150 pounds, soaking wet. His light brown hair is thin to begin with and receding significantly. There are pouches under his hazel eyes and lines around his thin lipped mouth. He has worked as an insurance adjuster for the past twenty years. Although he does not look like an erotic athlete, he refers to himself as a sexual conqueror.

I've always been into sex. When I was a younger fellow, I actually made a study of it. I read all the how-to books and examined all the anatomy charts they contained. I read Kinsey, Albert Ellis, Masters and Johnson, and all the other American sexologists. I guess I wanted my knowledge to give me the power that I lacked in my physique.

When I absorbed everything the western writers had to offer, I began looking into the eastern approaches: the Kama Sutra, the Perfumed Garden, and finally tantric sex. That was what really did it for me. By studying the techniques of tantra, I was able to hold back my orgasm while making love for hours. When I was in school, girls weren't all that interested in a guy who looked like me. But when I had managed to bed a few of them, word got around that I was a champion lover. After that, I was kept pretty busy, proving the rumors that were circulating about me. I never lacked a date or a sex partner when I wanted one.

Most of the time, in spite of what they heard, the women I went to bed with were surprised by my performance. I could keep thrusting forever, bringing them to orgasm after orgasm, without ever losing my erection. It takes work to master that kind of control, but believe me, it's worth it. There is nothing that turns me on quite so much as the cries of a woman having a climax. Even better are her words of praise and gratitude afterwards.

Most guys have to beg women for sex. In my case, it was just the opposite. Women would call me up and ask me out on dates or invite me to their apartments. They always knew they could count on me to give them multiple orgasms and complete satisfaction.

One night, when I was about twenty-five, I received a call from a woman I had never met before. Her name was Lynn. She said a friend of hers had given her my number. When she mentioned her friend's name, I knew that Lynn was calling me for sex. I had been with the friend only a week before, and she had asked if she could introduce me to someone she said was in desperate need of a good lover.

Lynn and I agreed to meet for a drink at a local cocktail lounge. I liked her from the start. She was a few years older than I and told me she had recently been divorced. She admitted frankly that her sex life during marriage had been a disaster. She said that her husband was only interested in himself. Not once in the entire course of her marriage had she ever gotten off by having sex with him. After the divorce, she had been out with a few men, but it was always pretty much the same story. She said that if it wasn't for her vibrator, she wouldn't have any sex life at all.

It was obvious that she was in need of a thorough loving. Since this was the reason for our date, I decided not to prolong her agony. I simply said, "Your place or mine?"

I supposed she might be a little startled by my directness, but if she was, she managed to cover it nicely. Without showing any sign of shock whatsoever, she answered, "Your place." Then she added, "As long as it isn't too far away." Even though she maintained her cool, the tremor in her voice showed how tense she really was. As we walked the short distance to my apartment, I was aware that she was extremely nervous, although she was trying hard not to show it. I actually felt her arm shaking in my grasp.

When we got inside, she turned and pressed herself against me, letting me know she was ready, but allowing me to take the initiative. I kissed her long and hard. My tongue's explorations of the inside of her mouth brought a long sigh of pleasure from her throat.

"Let's get undressed," I said softly. "Then we'll be free to make love without any obstacles to complete satisfaction."

I knew that sexual satisfaction was what she most craved, yet I saw a look of doubt flit across her face. She had never been satisfied by a partner before. In spite of whatever her friend had told her about me, she did not really think it was possible. But she was so hungry that she complied numbly with my suggestion.

I stepped back and watched as she anxiously removed her clothing. She was prettier than most of the women I had known, with long dark hair and big brown eyes. She had a wonderful figure, which was being revealed to me rather quickly as she stripped. When she was down to her underthings, I could see that her breasts filled the cups of her black satin bra. Her abdomen was flat, and there was a deep brown birthmark shaped like a miniature hand just above the waistband of her matching bikini panties.

She peeled off the bra and panties, standing naked before me, like some kind of supplicant. Her full breasts were capped with huge disks that were almost purple in color. There was a thick shock of hair growing all around her crotch. The birthmark seemed to be emerging from it.

I took her in slowly, my gaze moving from the top of her head to the toes of her bare feet. The sight of her aroused me as much as the fact that she was wordlessly begging for sexual release. In her desperation, she was counting on me to bring her a satisfaction that she had never known before and that she only had the vaguest notions about. It made me feel important and powerful.

I quickly removed my clothes and took her in my arms. Her big breasts pressed against my chest, empowering me further and making my erection stand up straight and hard. As we kissed, I began caressing her back lightly with the tips of my fingers. I let them trail around to the front so I could stroke the outside curves of her breasts. I was careful to be patient. I was in no hurry and wanted her to know that from the start.

"Why don't we go inside?" I suggested softly, leading her by the hand into my bedroom. With gentle pressure, I placed her on her back on the bed, positioning her with arms and legs slightly spread. "Relax," I whispered. "Leave everything to me."

I began touching and kissing her all over, as softly and as gently as I possibly could. When my lips brushed against her areolae, I felt and saw her nipples hardening. I kissed them lightly, just lapping their tips with the end of my tongue. With that, I felt the tension flowing out of her. She was beginning to believe. That turned me on intensely.

I continued kissing and lapping at her bare skin until I found my way to her dark bush of pubic hair. I nuzzled and sniffed the thickly curling down, filling my lungs with the air that wafted from the center of her sex. I began tasting her lips, feeling them swell and pout as my tongue worked its way over the sensitive pink membranes. She was moaning actively now. Her hips moved involuntarily, making little ovals as my mouth explored her opening.

Her clitoris was hard, its dark head peeping out from the tent of flesh that protected it. I licked at it lightly, feeling it throb in response to my touch. I continued licking and tasting her until I saw the little love button retreating again into its shell.

Some men think that means they have to lick harder to bring it out again, but I know better. My studies have taught me that when it goes back inside that way, the woman is getting close to orgasm. Direct pressure at that point is likely to irritate her and break the rising action, totally destroying the mood. So I began lapping around the swollen clitoral mound, touching the skin around it with the tip of my tongue, but never making direct contact with the sensitive little organ itself.

Within moments, she was coming. Her pelvis thrashed as the practiced movements of my tongue brought her deeper and deeper into climax. When she thought it was over, I kept working the outside of her clitoral hood with my tongue until I felt her climbing the plateau once again. I could tell from the gasping sounds she made as she came for the second time that this was a totally unexpected response for her.

Before she could recover from that orgasm, I mounted her, driving my swollen member deep into her waiting chamber. For a moment, I remained perfectly still, letting her sheath adapt and adjust to the intrusion. Then I began flexing the muscles of my groin, causing my organ to swell and relax, swell and relax, rhythmically inside her. I knew if I kept that up for a minute or two, she would come again, but she didn't know it.

She didn't think such pleasure was possible. She was trying to lift herself against me, to force me to begin the thrusting that most men think is what sex is all about. To her surprise, I timed the movements of my body to match hers, so that my penis remained in the same position inside her. Instead of pulling it in and out, I just kept flexing and expanding it.

Finally she realized what I was doing and relaxed again. As soon as she did, her third climax was upon her. I felt the contractions of her body announce its progress. Just before it ended, I did begin the thrusting she had been expecting. I was, of course, able to control my own responses totally so that I would not come until I decided the time was right. It wouldn't be right until she had experienced enough orgasms to make up for all the times she had been deprived.

I thrusted until she came again. Then I flexed for a while, until she came again. Then I remained perfectly still to let her vaginal muscles relax. Just when she thought it was finished, I began a twisting movement of my hips that made my penis rotate inside her, and she came yet again. And again. And again. Eventually, I lost count.

Finally, when she seemed about to collapse from total exhaustion, I relaxed the muscles of my pelvis and let my own orgasm occur. I knew she could feel me swelling and relaxing inside her as I filled her with my ejaculate. When I was spent, I let out a long, hoarse sigh.

"Thank you," she murmured. It was all she could say. We lay in each other's arms for an hour before either of us felt like moving. At last, she said, "You are the most incredible lover in the universe. I didn't know it was possible for a man to do for a woman what you have done for me."

Her words gave me more satisfaction than any of my own climaxes ever could. The knowledge that I had fulfilled her and made her happy filled me with pride. The superlatives she used in describing my sexual abilities made me feel like a true champion.

She continued singing my praises. She told me that she had almost been ready to give up on ever finding sexual satisfaction with a partner. She said she had been wondering whether it was all her fault, whether she might not be normal. She said I had freed her from those doubts.

As she spoke, I felt myself falling for her. When she said she was worried that she would never find another man who could please her this way, I answered, "Don't worry about that. I'll always be here for you." I guess I meant that she could call me any time, the way so many other women did. But as I said it, I realized that it sounded like the beginning of a serious relationship. In fact, that's what it turned out to be.

I saw Lynn every night for the next few weeks. When other women called me, I simply said I was busy, without promising to call them back. Eventually, Lynn moved in with me. I never tired of making love to her. She never stopped telling me how wonderful it was, what a great lover I was, how her satisfaction depended entirely on me. A year later, we were married.

Our marriage was idyllic for the first two years. She never lost her sexual appetite, and I never lost my tantric ability. I gave her multiple orgasms every time we made love. We made love just about every night. Afterward, she would go into raptures, telling me what a champion I was. It made me feel great.

When she became pregnant, we were both thrilled. After all, we weren't exactly kids anymore and didn't have that many reproductive years left. When our daughter was born, we were crazy about her. Of course, that didn't leave quite as much time for sex as we were used to, and we had to be careful not to wake the baby when we did manage to make love. But our sessions were still just as hot and passionate as ever.

Then, two years later, our second was born. A year and a half after that, we had our third. Almost overnight, Lynn had become a full-time mother and housewife. She managed to keep her figure, and I still longed to give her pleasure. But her sexual appetite began to change. Maybe it was the constant feeling that one of the kids needed her, or the fear that our sessions would wake them up. Perhaps she was worried about becoming pregnant again. I don't know.

All I do know is that we started doing it less and less often. The worst part was that when we did do it, she no longer craved lengthy lovemaking or multiple orgasms. She always seemed to be in a hurry to get it over with. She'd come once, within a couple of minutes, and immediately lose interest. She no longer praised my ability. Let's face it, there was nothing left for her to praise. I was still capable of performing tantric miracles that could satisfy a woman beyond belief, but I was getting no opportunity to demonstrate it.

In frustration, I decided to do something to get me out of the house a couple of evenings a week. So I signed up for a yoga class. I probably knew more about the subject than the instructor, but it was nice to get together with other people who were interested in eastern type body culture. It was there I met my new sex partner. Let's call her Alice. She's in the class with me.

One evening after class, Alice and I were chatting about Eastern mysticism in general and physical practices in particular. She asked if I had ever heard of tantric sex. I laughed. "Heard of it?" I echoed. "I'm an expert in it."

Alice said she had been reading about tantric exercises and the possibilities that they could result in multiple orgasms, but she had never met a man she could try it with. One thing led to another, and pretty soon we were at her place, fucking our brains out. Funny, I didn't use that kind of language till I met Alice, but she likes saying it, and now so do I.

She is in her early twenties and still very much in to sex. She says she loves the way I can get her off ten or twelve times in a row while holding back on my own climax until she is totally worn out. When our bouts of tantric lovemaking are over, she enjoys telling me what a sexpert she thinks I am. She calls me her gold-medal champion and says that without my loving, her life would be a wasteland. I lap up that kind of praise like nectar. It makes me feel the way I used to feel in my marriage.

Alice and I make no pretense of love or any sort of deep relationship at all. We just get together for secret sex. She gets one kind of satisfaction from it, and I get another. She has multiple orgasms, and I feel like a conqueror again.

THE SEX GODDESS

Meg, thirty-six, is dressed conservatively but exquisitely when we meet her, wearing a dark business suit over a white blouse with ruffles at the cuffs and collar. She is five feet nine inches tall, with the bearing and figure of a runway model. Her long legs are slender and her waist is trim. She is too curvy to be described as boyish, but there does not seem to be an ounce of spare flesh anywhere on her frame. Her light brown hair is short and elegantly coiffured. Her pale green eyes are accented by just a trace of makeup, expertly applied. She wets her full lips with quick movements of her tongue as she speaks softly but with confidence.

I live a very staid and conservative life. My husband is rather well-known in political circles, and I must maintain my spotless reputation. If he or his colleagues knew about my former lifestyle, or about the things I do now, I think they'd die of disbelief.

When I was younger, considerably younger, I used to run with a wild crowd of people. I came from money and could pretty much do whatever I wanted. My friends and I spent all our time drinking fine wine, smoking high-class marijuana, sniffing an occasional toot of cocaine, and partying. Some of the people in our group had their own planes, and we were always flying to the world's hottest spots to be in the right places at the right times when things were happening.

And the sex! Well, you just wouldn't believe the things that went on sexually.

For one thing, it was a very open group. What I mean is that pairing off or coupling up was strictly taboo. We had nothing but ridicule for people who got involved with one person on an exclusive basis. We even had a name for them. We called them sinkers, because once they were hooked, they just seemed to sink to the bottom of the world and remain out of sight forever.

We were all very good friends. It was understood that our

friendship carried over into the sexual arena as well. What that meant was that anybody in the group was free to have sex with anybody else in the group at just about any time, without anyone else thinking anything special about it. At our parties, we'd all have sex right out in the open, watching each other, changing partners in the middle of the act, even taking on multiple partners. I used to love having two or three men at once.

I remember one particular party we had at which someone came up with the brilliant idea of crowning a champion—the person who could have sex with the greatest number of partners at the same time. I'll never forget the fun I had winning that prize. I don't think I consciously set out to become champion. I just managed to excel in the multiple partners department.

We were on a yacht a few miles from one of the Greek islands and had the sea pretty much to ourselves. The sun was warm. All of us had been nude since the minute we sailed out of the harbor. When the action began, we were scattered all over the deck. My eyes were shut tight against the brightness of the sky.

I felt hands running over my bare skin. Fingertips plucked at my erect nipples. Palms stroked the swell of my breasts and caressed my belly. Fingers ran through my pubic hair and petted my pussy lips, parting them, letting the warm sea breeze waft over my inner tissues. The feeling was exciting. With my eyes closed, I had no idea who was touching me. I didn't even know whether the hands belonged to men or women. It made no difference.

I was tingling with desire. Reaching out blindly, I found another body next to mine and began exploring it. I could tell it was a male by the hardness of the muscles. My hand found its way down to his groin and the swollen staff of his cock. I grasped it lovingly and began stroking up and down.

My other hand found a woman. I explored her the same way, until my fingers were wet with the juices of her sex. I lay there, being stroked and petted by unknown lovers while with one hand I stroked a man's swollen prick and with the other I plunged a woman's pussy. It felt like heaven.

After a while, someone mounted me and a stiff prick found its way into my opening. I spread my legs wide and lifted them in the air, wrapping them around the waist of my unseen lover. At the same time, I felt two mouths sucking at my nipples, each with a different pressure, each with a different technique.

It only took a moment for the man who was screwing me to come. I felt him emptying himself inside me and then slipping out to make room for another. A moment later, a different cock penetrated me.

While my body was immersed in these erotic pleasures, my eyes remained closed. I did not know who was fucking me, who was sucking me, who was stroking me, who I was touching. That made the experience even more exciting. When the man who was on top of me finished, he was replaced by another, and then another. When I felt like coming, I came. When I thought I was spent, a new lover would bring me up again. I was swimming in a world of orgasm, drowning in a sea of semen.

I felt the head of a man's prick grazing the lips of my mouth and I opened it for him. As he entered me orally, I began licking and sucking, interested only in the exchange of sensations. I tongued and lapped until he came. I enjoyed the feeling of his cock pumping, going limp, and finally slipping from between my lips with a plop.

Next I felt the soft touch of a woman's genitals grazing my mouth. I began to lick and suck her as well. My tongue found her clit and worked it until I heard her groaning with ecstasy. The taste of her climax was fresh on my lips when she was replaced by another woman.

I was having one orgasm after another, as I paid lip service to the people who were lining up for satisfaction. Unknown cocks and tongues and fingers plundered my pussy. It seemed that the pleasure was endless, that the joy would never cease.

I don't have any idea how long the orgy continued. I know that the sky was bright when we started. It wasn't over until the sun was dropping into the beautiful waters of the Mediterranean. I have no notion of how many different partners had me and how many different partners I had that day. Somebody must have been keeping track, though, because I was unanimously proclaimed the champion.

After that I was known among our circle as the Sex Goddess. I don't mind telling you that I took some pride in the title. Everybody in our group was devoted to sex, yet I was uniformly acknowledged as the best of the best; the most promiscuous person in a crowd of promiscuous people.

I tried my best to live up to the reputation that went with my title. I was always searching for new and more creative ways to achieve sexual satisfaction. I was always the first to get out of my clothes at one of our gatherings. When a new man or woman was introduced to our crowd, I was usually the first to welcome him or her, with my mouth and my hands and my pussy. My whole body was devoted to sexual pleasure.

I lived this life of bliss for several years, filling my days and nights with recreational sex, recreational drugs, and recreational travel. But time was beginning to catch up with me. There really is something to that business about a biological clock. Mine was ticking. I was very much aware that the hours of idle pleasure were running out. I realized that I couldn't carry on this way forever. I knew that if I didn't stop soon, I would never be able to find a normal life.

I started spending less time with my indolent friends. Although I was in my late twenties, I decided to go to school. I won't mention the college, except to say that it's one of the best in the country. My family are big contributors, so I really could have gotten by without doing too much work, but I found myself becoming involved in and really enjoying my studies. It might not have been as much fun as the sun-swept orgies on yachts plying the Greek islands, but it was fascinating in a different way.

I majored in political science and received a degree. The year after my graduation, I campaigned for a presidential candidate. I don't think I'll identify him, except to say that he didn't win. I was assistant to a man named Franklin, the regional campaign manager. In some ways, we had a great deal in common, even though he was ten years older than I. We came from the same kind of social background. Our families had known each other for generations. We were acquainted with lots of the same people.

In other ways, we were as different as night and day. While I had been carousing with my wild and crazy crowd, Franklin had been devoting himself to politics and public service. I had put my efforts into achieving sexual satisfaction; he had put his into realizing his ambitions. He told me that he planned to be a U.S. Senator one day. He never thought he had time for anything else. He was practically a virgin when we met, having dated only a few women.

I resolved to change that. During the course of the campaign, we had dinner together a few times, but all he ever did was talk about politics. Eventually, it became obvious that our candidate was not White House bound, and he dropped out of the race. It was then that I insisted that Franklin and I go out on an actual date. Afterward, I made him invite me to his town house for a cocktail, which was where I seduced him.

He wasn't all that hard to seduce, having been sexually starved for most of his life. A few tender kisses were all it took. In no time at all, I had him in bed. I was a little surprised at how clumsy he was.

When I started to go down on him, it was obvious that he had never experienced anything like that before. He loved it but just didn't know how to act. When he was about to come, he got so confused that he almost lost it. He didn't know whether to pull my head away or to let it fly. I knew what was going on and just kept sucking until he had no choice but to let nature take its course.

Our sex life was an educational experience, with me doing all the educating. Sex was not a big priority for him, so I always had to be the one to initiate our encounters. He was far more interested in moving up the political ladder. I found satisfaction with him in a new kind of way.

With the old crowd, nothing had been special. Everybody was always very blasé about whatever was going on. With Franklin, every sexual experience was a new one. Each one of his orgasms was like a supernatural event. I was the angel who brought him to the doors of heaven.

After we had been seeing each other for a little more than a year, he asked me to marry him. I immediately said yes. There wasn't much excitement in our sex life, but that doesn't mean our marriage wasn't interesting. A few times a week we attended gatherings and get-togethers at which we rubbed elbows with some of the most powerful people in the state. Franklin was fast becoming one of them. When he was elected to his first office—and I don't think I'd better say which one it was—we moved to the state capital.

Political life kept me busy enough, but I did suffer from the lack of sexual adventure. Remember, I used to be a champion, the Sex Goddess. Now, I was lucky if I had sex once every two weeks. Even then, it was nothing to write home about. Nevertheless, I resolved to accept my new life. The prestige and status, I hoped, would eventually compensate for the pleasures I had lost.

One night, at a capital city cocktail party, I saw a familiar face in the crowd. It was Kendall, one of my old friends from the wild days. I could tell he spotted me at about the same time I noticed him. Slowly, we started working our way towards each other through the gathered politicians and hangers-on. We managed to meet at the bar.

"Why, hello, Meg," he said. "I saw your picture in the paper recently and had a feeling we'd be running into each other sooner or later."

"Nice to see you, Kendall," I answered. "I didn't know you were in politics."

"Well, I'm not really," he said, chuckling. "Some of my money is. Let's just say I'm a big supporter of some political causes."

"I didn't think you cared about causes," I said.

"I think of it as an investment," he answered. "I finance the causes that end up making me money. Not that I need more of it. It's just a game I play to get away from my wife."

"Oh?" I inquired. "You're married, then?"

"Of course," he said. "Most of our old crowd are sinkers now. None of them married each other. No, we've all picked rather dull mates and are living rather dull lives. Except for those rare occasions when we get together."

His words intrigued me. "You mean you're still in touch with the people we used to know?" I asked.

"Some of them," he said. "We party together whenever we can. It isn't the same though—not without our Sex Goddess."

I felt myself blushing. "I haven't been much of a Sex Goddess lately," I admitted. "My husband . . ."

"Oh, I know all about your husband," Kendall said. "He's one of the causes I invest in. Nice guy. Highly principled. I don't imagine he's very exciting in the bedroom, though." His voice got soft and reminiscent as he added, "Remember the good times we used to have?"

"Sometimes," I answered. "Sometimes I remember them so well that I don't know how I can go on with my present life." I had never expressed a thought like that before, not even to myself. "Sometimes I long for the old life."

"Maybe the next time we get together, you could join us," Kendall said.

"Oh, I'd love to," I answered wistfully. "But I couldn't take a chance of jeopardizing Franklin's career."

"We're all in that same boat," Kendall countered. "If anything happened to damage that husband of yours, I'd lose substantial money. Everybody else in the group is living the straight life, too. Nobody want to be exposed. We're all sinkers. You'll never find a more discreet group of people."

His words convinced me. A few weeks, later, he called to invite me to a reunion of old friends. Franklin was going to be out of town that night, so I didn't even have to make up an excuse.

The party was everything I hoped it would be. We all got naked almost as soon as we got into the house where we were meeting. After that, it was just like old times. I didn't keep track, but I think I had at least six partners. I felt like the old Sex Goddess again, champion of champions. It was good to see that all the years with Franklin hadn't made me lose my touch. I still could turn other men and women on and I still had the capacity for fabulous orgasms of my own.

Since then I've been getting together with my old friends every now and then. Re-experiencing the thrill of being the Sex Goddess has made my life with Franklin much easier to bear. Sometimes, I even find it relaxing to make love to him in a simple uncreative way. He holds a very important office now, and I am treated with respect wherever I go. I guess you could say I'm living in the best of two worlds.

$\mathcal{C}$ONCLUSION

In this book, we have told the stories of people who lead double lives. All are married or involved in permanent domestic partnerships. All engage or have engaged in clandestine sexual activity outside their primary relationships. In telling these stories, we do not intend to condone or recommend this behavior. Nor do we condemn it. We simply recognize that it exists and expect our readers to recognize that as well.

The stories are divided into twelve chapters, each offering a reason for the secret sex of the people telling the stories. We do not promise, however, that reasons given are the genuine motivations for the behavior involved. We do not know what drives the subjects of the stories to act the way they do. We only know what they claim to be the forces behind their infidelity.

Some of their explanations appear, on their face, to be concocted for the purpose of justifying conduct about which the participants themselves feel guilty. For example, Nelson, the university professor, says he thinks his outside affairs strengthen his marriage. Yet he admits that similar affairs destroyed two of his previous relationships. After discovering spanking games with an old friend, Joan says that her husband is much too serious to engage in that kind of sex play. Yet there is no indication that she ever asked him to do so or otherwise attempted to solicit his co-operation.

On the other hand, some informants seem to be making honest attempts at self-understanding. Megan, who has indiscriminate sex with customers after cutting their hair, frankly admits that she isn't marriage material, that "forsaking all others till death do us part" just isn't for her, that one man will never be enough. Monica, a forty-six-year-old self-styled housewife, concedes that she hates the idea of aging and explains her affair with the young man who maintains her swimming pool by saying that it makes her feel vintage instead of old.

We think the fact that the people who told us their stories act the way they do is much more important than the reasons they gave us for their actions. We also think it likely that most people have some sexual secrets, and that many carry on secret sex lives. If you are one of them, you have probably come up with reasons for your own infidelity. The explanation you give yourself may be genuine or it may be contrived. Perhaps examining the reasons stated by others will help you realize the truth about your own.

A song that was popular some years ago asked the question "Who's making love to your old lady while you're out making love?" If you have a secret sex life, that may be a question worth asking yourself, in whatever form is appropriate to your gender. Can it be that you are not the only one in your relationship who has found a reason to look for sexual fulfillment on the outside? If so, are you willing to go on that way, or would you like to change your life?

We are not qualified or licensed to offer advice about relationships and, even if we were, we would not feel comfortable doing so. However, we would be missing an important point if we neglected to mention that there are many people who have taken the secrecy out of their sexual behavior and learned to share special erotic needs with their mates. This calls for a degree of honesty that some find frightening, and it certainly doesn't work for everyone. But it might be something worth considering.

If your reasons for extrarelationship sexuality are based on what you perceive as your partner's unwillingness to do the kinds of things you like, ask yourself whether you are sure that this is so. Have you ever frankly discussed your desires with him or her? If so, was the refusal ironclad? Instead of assuming that there is no hope, try discussing and negotiating, the way you would if you disagreed about the color of the next family car you were planning to buy.

Remember, though, that sexual differences are not one-sided. Your spouse or partner may have some needs that she or he thinks you are unwilling to fulfill. Consider these, too, and see whether you can find a way to be comfortable with them. Recognize that if you cannot, your mate may go looking for someone who can, as the people have done whose stories are told in this book.

A serious discussion of sexual differences may enhance your relationship and bring you a new happiness free of frustration and guilt. If that happens, we'd like to hear about it. Write to us and tell us about your intimate experiences. We may repeat your story for the benefit of others, but we will never reveal your identity.

ATTENTION READERS

The authors have already begun gathering information for their next book. If you would like to participate by filling out a questionnaire, please write to them at:

Iris and Steven Finz
P.O. Box 237
The Sea Ranch, CA 95497

Or e-mail them at:

huck@sexwriters.com

Or visit their Web site for information and a questionnaire:

www.sexwriters.com

/5𝑜

BORED BY THE
MONOTONY OF MONOGAMY?

"Earl and I have gotten together every few weeks for sex in the afternoon. I don't think my marriage is the least bit threatened by it. In fact, I think it has been a definite improvement. I love Rennie and I love making love with him. But there's something about having a secret sex life that makes our relationship all the more exciting."

—Glenda, 31

"Now, making love with Barbara has become a kind of ritual that we practice after each lesson. It's more sex than I have with Charles. And better, too . . . I know I'm still a heterosexual woman. I like having a husband. I like being married. But the sex I have with my female lover is the best I can imagine."

—Suzanne, 40

"I hated to see Brett leave and wondered whether it would ever happen again. Well, it has. Almost every time he comes to service the pool. Frederick doesn't suspect a thing. I'm not even sure whether he realizes that his wife is happier and has become a better lover to him. But I know I am. And I think I owe it all to my affair with Brett."

—Monica, 46

ALSO BY
IRIS AND STEVEN FINZ

Unspoken Desires
Erotic Confessions
What Turns Us On
The Best Sex I Ever Had
Whispered Secrets

AVAILABLE FROM
ST. MARTIN'S PAPERBACKS

IRIS AND
STEVEN FINZ

$\mathcal{S}$ECRET

SEX

REAL PEOPLE TALK ABOUT
THEIR MOST SECRET FANTASIES
AND SEX LIVES

St. Martin's Paperbacks

SECRET SEX

Cover photo by Greg Weiner.

Library of Congress Catalog Card Number: 2001054823

ISBN: 0-312-98671-8

Printed in the United States of America

St. Martin's Press hardcover edition / March 2002
St. Martin's Paperbacks edition / February 2003

St. Martin's Paperbacks are published by St. Martin's Press, 175 Fifth Avenue, New York, NY 10010.

10 9 8 7 6 5 4 3 2 1